Gardening with Your Head in the Clouds

Gardening with Your Head in the Clouds: A Weather Primer for Gardeners

Illustrated by Stacey Leonard
Edited by Robin Catalano

Book design by The Troy Book Makers
Printed in the United States of America
The Troy Book Makers • Troy, New York • thetroybookmakers.com

To order additional copies of this title,
contact your favorite local bookstore
or visit www.shoptbmbooks.com

ISBN: 978-1-61468-921-8

Gardening with Your Head in the Clouds

A Weather Primer for Gardeners

Alicia Wasula, PhD

Foreward

I first met Alicia in a cozy coffee shop in upstate New York back in 2018. We were meeting for an interview for me to join her meteorological consulting firm, and I was nervous! However, her kindness instantly put me at ease, and we easily settled into conversation. Over the next several years, Alicia quickly evolved from a stranger to a colleague, mentor, and friend. Though I have since moved out of state, I was always delighted when Alicia shared treats from her garden with me when we lived a few miles apart.

In a dynamic and interdisciplinary field that continues to evolve and grow, Alicia is a steady beacon and guiding force for good. She serves as a leader and mentor in many official and unofficial capacities, both within the meteorological community and her local community. Her guiding principles of clear communication and sound science shine throughout this book.

I've had the pleasure of witnessing the passion and love that Alicia has poured into this book, and I am confident that all who read it will be glad they did. Weather for Gardeners is a testament to Alicia's wealth of knowledge and way with words. Whether you are a seasoned gardener looking to learn more about the world around you or simply someone who wants to dive into the world of weather, Alicia breaks down the complex topics of our atmosphere in a completely accessible and easy-to-understand format, with anecdotes and insights sprinkled throughout. Her skill in distilling indisputably intricate topics into digestible bites is unparalleled, making this a must-read not only for meteorologists and weather enthusiasts, but also for gardeners, students, or anyone who is a lover of the great outdoors.

Whether you are curious about how to begin observing the weather in your own backyard, looking to become more informed on how to prepare for different extreme weather events, or eager to read a non-biased summary about climate change, Alicia will cover all of these topics in addition to answering many other common weather-related questions such as, "Why is the sky blue?"

I encourage you to immerse yourself in the book, taking time to really look at the photographs and figures within. Highlight, take notes, dog-ear the pages, insert sticky notes on parts you want to come back to time and time again. Use the Weather Notes template in the Appendix to get started on your own weather exploration journey. Understanding the relationship between weather and gardening is an integral part of becoming a successful gardener. I am confident this book will answer many questions to help you become more aware of the environment around you, leading you to make more informed decisions, resulting in healthier and more productive gardens. Even if you aren't a gardener (guilty, although this book may have inspired me to give it a try!), this book is a fantastic read that I believe anyone interested in the environment will enjoy.

Happy reading!

Kelly Cebulko

Dedication

This book is dedicated to Nonni, my Italian grandma
who taught me that growing and cooking food for your family
with your own hands is one of the greatest ways you can love them.

*Nonni passing her love of gardening on to the next generation,
my children (then ages 2 and 6; Summer 2010).*

Table of Contents

Chapter 3: Summer 69

Chapter 4: Autumn 105

Introduction

Gardening has been a part of my life for as long as I can remember. My grandmother, who lived just outside of New York City, kept an amazing garden. My memories of visiting her in the spring and summer months always involved fresh vegetables and fruits. At every meal, after we had our pasta—usually served with home canned tomato sauce—she served a fresh-from-the-garden salad, a simple mix of lettuce, tomatoes, and cucumbers lightly dressed with oil, vinegar, and a little salt and pepper. With a slice of homemade bread, I would mop up the last bits from my plate. Although I was a terribly picky eater, I gobbled up her home-grown zucchini that she made into a delicate pasta sauce. Her marinade for grilled chicken, made with pureed basil, other herbs, and plenty of garlic, was legendary.

When we were kids, Nonni would always walk my brother and me through the garden to see her tomatoes, squash, beans, and other vegetables (Photo 1). Maybe it was her way of trying to encourage me to become less picky, or because of the pride she took in growing her own food, or because she wanted to pass down her knowledge and life skills to her grandchildren. Whatever the reason, Nonni, her garden, and her amazing cooking are inseparable in my memories.

Photo 1: The author eating tomatoes off the vine as a young child.

My father also had a garden nearly every year when I was growing up. Although it was much smaller in scale than his mother's, we would grow some tomatoes, and sometimes beans, herbs, and other vegetables. I watched him dig out a patch in the spring, sow plants carefully chosen from our local nursery around Memorial Day, and then, by late summer, I was eating cherry tomatoes directly off the vines. I "helped" my dad tie up beans, stake tomatoes, and, my least favorite part, pull weeds. At the end of the season, we (he, mostly) would pull everything out and clean up the garden for the winter. From him I learned a lot of the routine tasks of keeping a vegetable garden.

My first job in high school was at our local nursery, where I learned how to grow and transplant seedlings, which plants and flowers grow best at which times of the year, how to mulch and fertilize, and how to water everything from seed trays to hanging baskets. I held that job throughout high school and summers when I was off from college. I always felt accomplished when I came home at the end of a shift, dirty, physically tired, and a little sunburned. Although my boss was difficult and often corrected me—too much water, not enough water, too much pruning; there was always something to improve on—I felt like I had finally earned my place on his staff when he allowed me to plant the flower arrangements at the very front of the parking lot, the displays that first greeted shoppers as they pulled in.

Although I remember enjoying gardening since my early childhood, I cannot say that I always knew I wanted to be a meteorologist. It is a rare person in our field who did not know as a child that they were meant to study the weather! I always enjoyed science, specifically physical sciences like astronomy, geology, and meteorology, but it was not until late high school that I considered meteorology as a college major. The fact that meteorology could be applied directly to real-world situations, such as knowing which plants to plant at what times of year, was what really drew me in and gave me the motivation to push through the difficult math and physics which is needed in this field.

As I grew into an adult and became a first-time home owner, I was thrilled when my husband agreed to build me two raised beds for our small yard. Each year my dad, who lived nearby, and I would discuss whether it was too early to plant our tomatoes, how the weather was affecting our plants, which varieties of plants were the best, and when it was time to clean up for the winter. When I visited my grandmother, I always came home with fresh veggies, flower and plant clippings from her garden to try out in my own yard, and tips and ideas for how to grow plants and save seeds.

Raised Bed Construction

Building a raised garden bed can be as simple or complex as one desires. When my husband built my first beds, I did a great deal of research on how best to construct them. I learned that it is favorable to use hardwoods such as cedar or pine for the beams. This ensures longevity and inhibits warping. Cedar beams can be quite expensive, so we chose pine. I also learned that pressure-treated beams should not be used, because the chemicals used in the pressure-treating process can leach into the soil.

We chose to build two rectangular beds four feet wide by eight feet long, which made cutting the beams to size easy. First, we carefully leveled the ground at the site of each bed. Construction was quite simple: we inserted a two-by-two square post into the ground at each corner, and then attached the beams at ground level to those posts. Some people line their raised beds prior to filling; I did not. I ordered about three yards of garden soil from our local farm and, a little at a time, filled up the bed with healthy soil. I did need to add soil and compost the second year, as compaction was significant the first year.

Although constructing a basic raised bed like mine is a very simple process, if you're handy, you can create more complex and artful garden beds. Some are built to be a few feet high, so the gardener can work without having to bend over. This is a good option for gardeners with mobility issues, but it does require a tremendous amount of soil to fill a deep raised bed. Trim and details can be added to create a custom look, as well.

If you are looking for an easy, fuss-free garden bed option, I recommend galvanized metal frames. These frames are available on Amazon and at some gardening centers, and are made up of ridged sheets of galvanized metal. The kits come with all the screws needed for assembly, and are super simple to install: simply screw together the panels and set in place. I like these because they are a little deeper than my original raised beds built from pine planks, plus the metal has held up very well over the years; by the time we sold our first house and moved, the raised beds at my old house were in severe need of an update, as the boards had warped and begun to rot over three to four winters.

Maintenance of raised beds is simple. In the fall, when I pull out my garden, I rake the beds flat. Sometimes I add compost, but some years I don't. Then I cover the beds with a thick layer of straw mulch. In the spring, I rake off the mulch, add some garden soil and compost, turn the soil a bit, and the beds are ready to go for planting!

As a trained scientist, it was only natural that I started keeping a garden journal shortly after I began keeping my own garden. My brain constantly took notes and made observations each time I was outside working, and I began writing quick notes of these observations down in a little notebook. My garden journals are not fancy; I use a simple notebook and write down quick notes. I do this as soon as I come inside so I don't forget my thoughts, so these little notebooks are well loved: dirty, crinkled from being wet, and full of reflections, plans, and observations ranging from weather conditions to how many critters I saw eating my lettuce.

Many home gardeners keep journals and make observations about weather conditions—cold snaps, drought, heavy rains, and late-season snow—which is essential to success as a gardener. I realized somewhere along the way that, because gardeners are such observant folks, they likely have many questions about how the weather "works." Why is there a rainbow after that summer thunderstorm? Why did it get so windy? Why is the snow that fell this week so heavy to shovel, while the snow that fell last month was fluffy and light? I have written this book with the home gardener in mind—those of us who don't have to rely on the fruits of our labors to feed our families, but who enjoy the challenge and hard work of trying to create beauty and function in our backyard flower and vegetable gardens.

In these pages, I will answer some of the most common weather questions that gardeners, or really anyone who spends time observing the outdoors, may have. These topics will not be discussed in a scientifically exhaustive, college-textbook style; for an introductory meteorology course, look to your local community college. Rather, this book will be peppered with personal reflections, visuals, and anecdotes to help illustrate meteorological concepts every gardener should know.

I have divided this book into four chapters, one for each season. In each chapter, I discuss weather topics that are applicable to that time of year. Topics are thus not presented in the typical sequential order found in most beginning meteorology textbooks. I also will devote some time discussing how to help you take detailed weather observations in your own yard. Finally, I will share many photos I have taken over the years of weather phenomena and my garden. At the end of each chapter is a section called 'Gardener Goals,' which includes some practical ways that you can gain a deeper understanding of weather and how it affects you and your garden.

I hope you can relate to all of the successes, as well as the many learning opportunities these photos document. If gardening isn't a journey that parallels life, I don't know what is. I hope this book helps you understand just a little bit more of the weather that so influences your gardening journey, and helps you enjoy and appreciate the process all the more.

Chapter 1

Winter

Winter "Gardening": Planning and Patience

Winter is the worst time of the year for gardeners. At my home in the northeast United States, winter after the holidays can be cold, gray, and dreary. Yes, we have snowstorms and the occasional sunny day, but sometimes we also have ice, sleet, rain, and wind. To make matters worse, everything is covered in a layer of road salt that just seems to get into every nook and cranny. However, just like in life, when things seem at their darkest, little glimmers of light appear.

I like to call this part of the year the "imagination gardening" time.

As I walk around my yard in the winter, I do a lot of thinking and planning inside my head. Which plants do I think won't make it through the winter? Which areas are going to get the first extra care come spring? What do I want to add to this section or that? Having long ago released the pressure of perfection, I am no longer afraid to think about making big changes, taking out plants that didn't work well, trying new plants just to see what will happen, and envisioning my yard as a place full of potential.

My gardening year usually starts with the arrival of seed catalogs. This year, they began arriving right on New Year's Day—a perfect time to think about a fresh start and get motivated by all the beautiful pictures in the catalog. I have both a small vegetable garden comprised of raised beds, as well as several spots in my yard where I grow flowers: perennials, annuals, and shrubs. Nothing is off-limits as I browse through the pages.

My first step is to dog-ear pages with interesting varieties of plants and make a list. This list usually contains far more types of vegetables than I could ever hope to grow in the space which I have, and also many types of flowers, some of which I know will never thrive in my soil but I can't help thinking I can somehow convince to grow. After much paring down, the final list of seeds usually contains varieties of old stand-bys, and just a few new varieties to try out.

Just like Nonni, I also save seeds. In January and February, I am often sorting through my seeds from past years. I remember watching Nonni dry out tomato seeds on the kitchen counter on a paper towel, and growing a whole garden completely from a previous garden—something I always found amazing. She saved seeds for tomatoes (many types), basil, peppers, zucchini, beans, and more. Sometimes her friends and neighbors would trade seeds, and so she always had some new variety of vegetable growing each year.

Seed saving is a much more daunting prospect for me than it ever was for Nonni. Knowing when to harvest the seeds, how to dry and preserve them, and how long to keep them for has always been a bit of a mystery to me. I find myself researching the 'how to' every year, no matter how many times I try it. And every spring, I am always surprised when I see that it actually worked, and my saved seeds germinate. I typically buy a couple of seed packets 'just in case' what I have saved doesn't take. Maybe someday saving seeds will come as naturally to me as it did to Nonni, but for now that reassurance of purchasing new 'just in case' seeds gives me the confidence to keep trying.

Once March arrives, spring is in the air even if the weather doesn't feel like it. The sun is getting stronger, daylight is increasing, and there are usually buds on the trees. March is when I start my inside seed trays. When I worked at the nursery in high school, one of my first tasks was transplanting seedlings from tiny little plug trays into the larger six-pack trays that are commonly found in garden centers. Inside the warm greenhouse, these thousands of little tiny sprouts would grow into plants by the time customers were looking for them; something I looked forward to each year.

The end of winter is also when I take specific notice of the weather patterns with respect to my garden, and look back through my journal to assess the year-to-year variability, and which plants performed best. Some cold-loving plants, such as lettuce, carrots, broccoli, and peas, can be sowed directly into the ground as soon as the soil can be worked. Some years I have seeds in the ground before the end of March. Other years the snow and ice just will not quit; I have sown the first outdoor seeds as late as April 20.

The appearance of buds on my potted fig tree also marks the beginning of the end of winter. Nonni had beautiful fig trees in her garden on Long Island. The marine climate was mild enough that they could be planted right in the ground and survive the winter, although she would wrap them up well to insulate them. Here in upstate New York, my family and I tried countless times over the years to propagate a clipping from one of her fig trees. Each year, my father would tip the small tree down, dig a long trench, and bury it for the winter. Inevitably, the fig tree would grow to a point where it became too big to tip over and bury, and would die after a harsh winter.

Maybe it is because every Italian gardener I have known has fig trees, maybe it is because of visions of the warm, sunny Mediterranean climate that the sight of a fig tree evokes, or maybe it is because there is nothing like the taste of a fresh fig picked off the tree (1)—whatever the reason, having a successful fig tree has always been a garden bucket-list item for me. Although I was never able to make Nonni's tree clippings work, I purchased some small potted fig tree clippings from a local nursery, Valoze's, which is owned by an Italian family. The fig plant was brought over from Italy with the original owners and is still in the greenhouse today. Cuttings from the original tree are sold each year in pots.

After some trial and error with Valoze's fig tree cuttings, I have come up with a system that is very labor intensive, but works. The tree lives in a gigantic pot on my patio. During the warm season, I water it regularly, fertilize it as needed, and it produces plentiful figs every September. As soon as the leaves fall off, my husband helps me load the entire pot onto a wagon and wheel it into its winter home in the back of the garage, to wait until its buds emerge in the spring. The tree requires very little care in the winter—no water, no cover, and just a small amount of sunlight. The back of the garage seems to be a moderate enough temperature with just enough light to keep the tree comfortable. Every year, it feels like a miracle when I first see tiny green buds on the tree.

The day we drag the fig tree out of the garage into the spring sun is a benchmark for me. The tree must be reacclimated slowly, usually by taking the heavy pot in every night to protect it from the cold for several weeks. Once the danger of frost has passed, we wheel it out onto the patio for the summer.

Fig Trees, Gardens, and Italian Culture

Gardens, particularly home gardens, have long been a part of Italian culture, and many Italians who immigrated to the United States brought this tradition, as well as saved seeds, with them (2) (3). Out of necessity, Italian homes in and around large cities like New York City often contained more garden area than lawn. Commonly grown produce included tomatoes, eggplant, basil, oregano, garlic, zucchini and other types of squash (including the tremendously long and unwieldy cucuzza (4)), peppers, and lettuce. Depending on the climate, other foods, such as grapes and artichokes, could be grown as well.

In an interview with La Cucina Italiana, author of the website The Italian Garden Project, Mary Menniti, notes that one of the hallmarks of Italian-American gardens is the presence of arbors, trellises, rain barrels, and other items crafted from repurposed materials. There was no need to purchase special tomato stakes when one could use old pieces of baseboard or leftover wood from a project. Plants were not tied up with fancy plastic clips, but rather bits of torn-up sheets and old rags. These practical elements give Italian gardens their character and charm.

Menniti devotes a great deal of space to the fig tree and its special place in Italian and Italian-American culture. The fig tree grows readily in Italy and other Mediterranean countries. Fig trees typically produce one crop at the end of the summer, and the fruit can be eaten right off the tree, or dried and saved for later use (5). Menniti notes that, as was the case with the Valoze greenhouse owners from whom I got my fig tree, many immigrants brought with them a clipping of their fig tree to cultivate here in their new home. These trees, like many of the seeds which traveled to America with immigrants, not only served the practical purpose of providing food for a family, but also created a direct link to the land, family, and culture they had left.

However, fig trees thrive in the warm Mediterranean climate, which does not have the harsh winters we have in the Northeast and other parts of the United States. Even on Long Island, where the climate is influenced by the warm Gulf Stream current, winters can be too cold for delicate fig trees. This is why it's necessary to bury or otherwise protect the plants during the cold months, as did Frank Miceli, who is featured on the Italian Garden Project website.

Frank is a native of Oswego, New York, on the shore of Lake Ontario in the lake effect snow belt, which averages 140 inches of snow per year. Daily average temperatures in the winter are well below freezing, and even in the summer months, the average daily high temperature is just under 80 degrees Fahrenheit.

Frank recollects the process of digging a large hole in front of his father, Carmelo's, fig tree. Friends and neighbors would help bend it into the ground and cover it. The tree was then raised, "as if from the grave," each spring and produced fruit every year. Having experienced many unsuccessful attempts with my family to bury fig trees in upstate New York, I was surprised and impressed that the Micelis were able to keep the fig tree alive through the harsh Oswego winters and relatively cool summers, which are influenced by breezes off of the lake.

Winter Topic #1: Seasons

Humans in all cultures and climates have, from the beginning, marked seasonal changes and built their lives around the rhythm of natural cycles. Growing up and living in an area of the world with four distinct seasons, I have always been very sensitive to their annual cycle. As winter recedes, those early warm spells, longer days, and brand-new green growth emerging from the ground heighten my anticipation. The same thing happens every year as summer wanes. The longer shadows at the end of the day and chill in the night air always make me look forward to apple picking, beautiful foliage, and those absolutely perfect warm days followed by cool nights.

Paying close attention to seasonal changes, particularly in the spring when things are just getting going in the garden, is important so we don't plant too early or too late—and I have done both! Maybe you live in the desert Southwest where the climate has two primary seasons, wet and dry, or maybe you live in a marine climate like that of the Pacific Northwest where temperatures are cool in the summer and relatively mild in the winter. No matter where you live, understanding why we have seasons at all can make a big difference in gardening success.

First, let's imagine ourselves as observers of the solar system from space. As we look at the solar system, the sun is at the center and Earth is moving in two primary ways. The first, called *revolution*, refers to how the earth moves in a nearly circular path around the sun. Earth completes one full revolution every 365.25 days; this is what gives us the length of our year (adjusted every four years with a leap year so that we are in the same position in our orbit around the sun at the same time of year). The second type of motion, which is called *rotation*, refers to the earth spinning on its axis like a ball spinning on the finger of a basketball player. The Earth completes one full rotation every twenty-four hours, and it is this movement that gives us the length of our day (Figure 1).

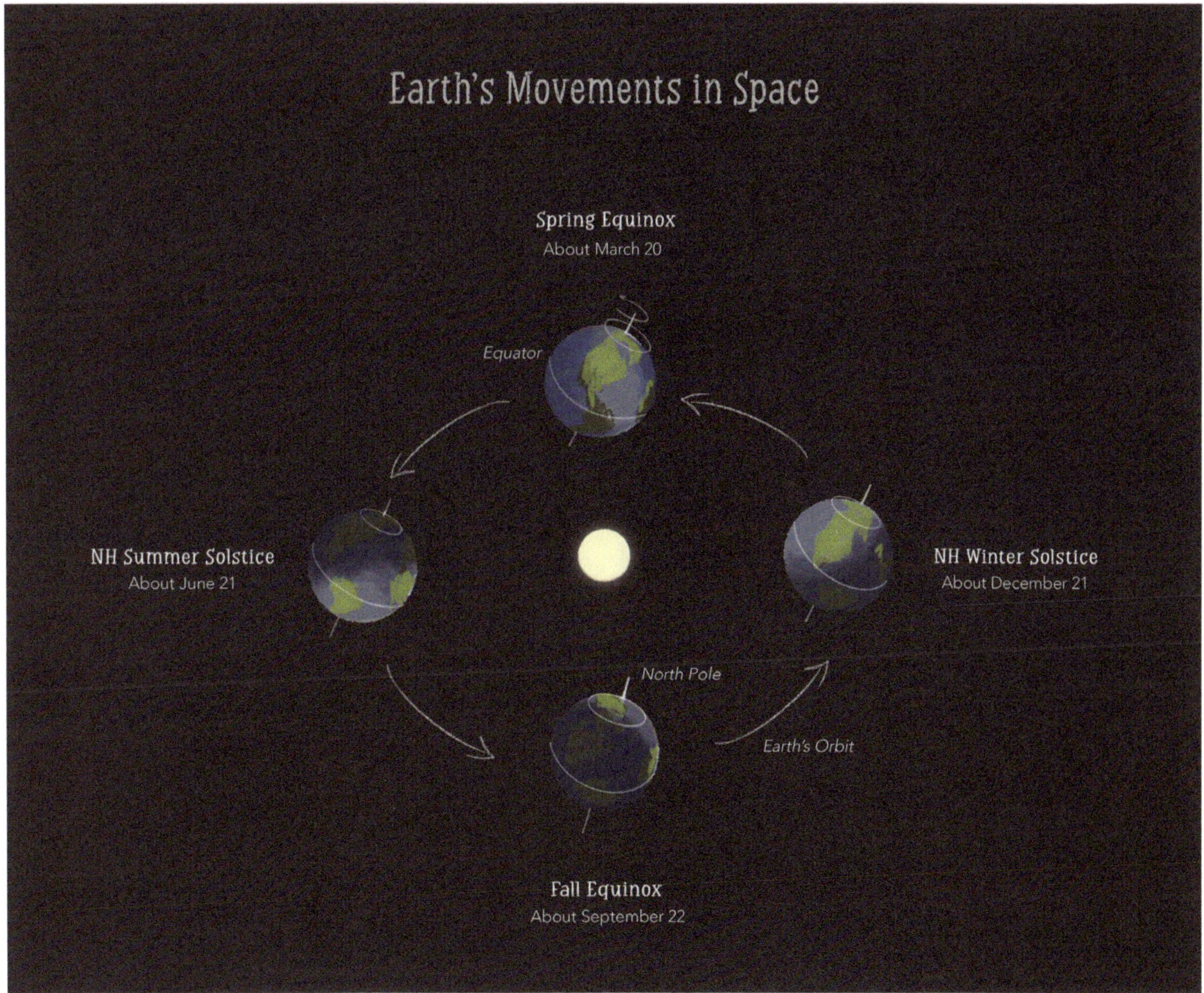

Figure 1

Whichever half of the earth faces the sun is in daytime; the half of the Earth facing away from the sun is in nighttime. The axis of Earth's rotation is a line which runs through the North and South poles, and the equator is an imaginary line around the center of the Earth exactly halfway between the poles. Visualize the Earth spinning like a top on its axis, revolving slowly around the sun once per year. Now consider this: the Earth's axis is not oriented vertically when viewed from the sun, but rather is tipped or tilted (Figure 2) 23.5 degrees off vertical.

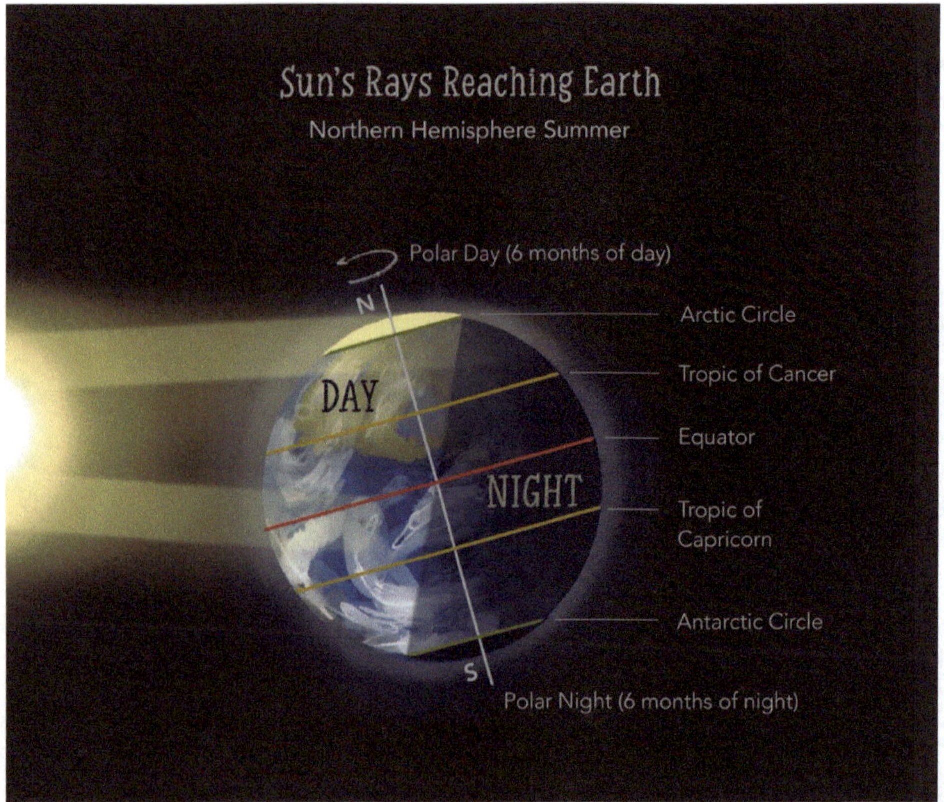

Figure 2

Why is this important? The reason we have seasons on Earth is because of the tilt of the Earth's axis. The net effect of this tilt is that certain parts of the Earth face the sun more directly, while others are tipped away from it. Wherever you are located, summer marks the warmest and longest days of the year, higher humidity, and a higher likelihood of getting a sunburn.

The energy that warms the Earth comes from the sun, which you can imagine as a giant flashlight directing a beam of light right at the Earth. When a flashlight is held vertically, perpendicular to the ground, it creates a narrow, intense beam of light. Now imagine that the flashlight is tipped at an angle closer to horizontal. The light beam is less intense, and spread out over a wider area. During the summer, the sun is higher in the sky during the day, which is analogous to the direct flashlight beam. The more direct rays, or radiation, more effectively heat the Earth's surface and atmosphere. During the winter, the sun is lower in the sky and the radiation is much less direct, and less effective at heating the Earth. However, when this weak radiation is bounced, or reflected, off of white surfaces such as fresh snow, sunburn is still possible, which is why it is so important to use sun protection while doing outdoor winter activities such as skiing. We'll get into more detail about humidity changes between seasons later, but for now, keep in mind that warmer air can contain more water vapor (the invisible gaseous form of water) than cold air can, and the presence of water vapor in the atmosphere creates the feeling of humidity.

Let's think in a little more detail about how the movement of the Earth in space through the seasons affects the length of days. In the Northern Hemisphere, our meteorological winter season is from December through February, which differs slightly from the astronomical definition of winter, which runs from the December solstice (usually around December 21) through the spring equinox in mid-March.

One of the first markers of spring that I notice is that the sun rises earlier and sets later. The days may still be cold, but the strength of the sun and the length of daylight in March are markedly different than in January. The shortest day of the year in the Northern Hemisphere is on the December solstice. The Northern Hemisphere is directed away from the sun and receiving weak or indirect radiation at this time. Conversely, in the summer months, the Northern Hemisphere is receiving more direct radiation and is exposed to that radiation for a longer period of time (longer days). The length of day depends on where one is located: close to the equator, there is comparatively little variability in day length from summer to winter, while areas north of the Arctic Circle (in the Northern Hemisphere) have extreme variability in day length. The areas near the poles receive no daylight for a period of time around the winter solstice, and no darkness for a time near the summer solstice in mid-June.

Here at my latitude in New York, we range from approximately nine hours of daylight during the winter to about 15 hours of daylight during the summer. The rate at which the length of day changes is variable as well. Although the shortest day of the year is in late December, the days really don't begin to feel longer until late February. By March and April, we rapidly gain more daylight each day, and then the rate of increase slows, although the days get slightly longer right up through the summer solstice in June.

Varying Length of Day at the Solstices

All areas of the Earth experience shorter days in the winter and longer days in the summer. How long or short those days are varies by location. The length of day over the course of a year changes the least for areas that are close to the equator, while regions near the poles see dramatic swings in the length of day over the course of the year.

For example, in Quito, Ecuador, located nearly on the equator, the length of daylight between sunrise and sunset (approximately 12 hours) varies only by about one minute during a year. In Orlando, Florida, the length of daylight ranges between about 10.5 hours in December to nearly 14 hours in June. Near the Arctic Circle in Juneau, Alaska, the difference between June and December daylight is even more pronounced: from under 6.5 hours in December to nearly 18.5 hours in June!

Barrow, Alaska, is even farther north than Juneau, and is located north of the Arctic Circle. Here, the sun sets around December 20 and does not rise again until January 23 or

24. During this time, the length of day in Barrow is zero! Conversely, the sun rises around June 10 or 11, and does not set again until late July or early August, which means the length of daylight is over seven weeks long!

One of the things you can do as a gardener, if you don't already, is to try to become more attuned to the seasonal changes in your area. If you wake up at the same time each day, notice how much daylight there is, and how long it takes the sun to rise. How long does twilight, the period between darkness and full daylight, last? What does the sun feel like on your face when you go outside? If you are outdoors around noon, the time when the sun is highest in the sky, notice its location—it will be much higher during the summer than in the winter (the difference is more exaggerated if you are far north of the equator). What about sunrise and sunset? Notice where in the sky the sun dips below the horizon while you enjoy those last few minutes of daylight on your patio each night.

There are regional differences to be aware of, as well. If you travel out of town to somewhere warm during the winter, observe the changes in these patterns, as they can be quite noticeable when you travel by plane from one climate to another. Paying close attention to seasonal changes in length of day, sunrise and sunset times, and how high the sun is in the sky, which are predictable and cyclical, will help you stay in tune with your garden's development. Wildlife such as insects, birds, and even mammals pay close attention to markers of the seasons, and as gardeners we can learn from them!

Growing in the Arctic

The length of the growing season is a metric that gardeners everywhere pay close attention to, and there are many ways to define a growing season (6). Whether one is a home gardener or a large-scale farmer, the number of days over a year when plants will grow determines what types of plants will thrive—but as both gardeners and meteorologists know, there is more than one reason why a plant will or will not grow. Yearly variations in the growing season, whether in the form of a late frost or an early freeze, can make or break the success that gardeners have growing crops.

Gardening in areas such as Alaska and northern Canada brings about a unique set of challenges. The growing season is much shorter than in more temperate regions. For example, in Anchorage, in southern Alaska, the average last frost is on May 7, while the average first frost is on September 24. This translates to a growing season of just 139 days. Farther to the north in Fairbanks, the average growing season is even shorter at 112 days, with the average first-frost date of May 16 and last-frost date of September 6. While the days can be very long, even close to 24 hours, the sunlight is relatively weak due to the low sun angle. This can cause bolting of leafy greens such as lettuce and spinach (7).

As one might expect, human intervention and technology is often required to be a successful gardener in an Arctic climate. It is necessary to carefully choose varieties of plants that can withstand the long days, weak sun, and large temperature swings. Greenhouses and grow lights can help to amplify the sun's light and extend the natural growing season. Although this climate is a challenge, networks such as the Master Gardeners and Cooperative Extension are able to help gardeners learn necessary skills and answer questions (8) (9).

Winter Topic #2: The Greenhouse Effect

You are no doubt familiar with the effect that a greenhouse has on temperature. Greenhouses and cold frames (small structures used for sheltering plants directly on the ground) trap incoming solar radiation inside the glass or plastic, increasing the interior temperature and allowing us to start plants much earlier in the spring than would otherwise be possible in cold climates. At my high school job at the plant nursery, I recall being grateful anytime I was assigned work inside the greenhouses when it was cold outside!

You may have heard of the term *greenhouse effect,* sometimes in conjunction with the term *global warming*. We will take a closer look at both of these terms later on and see why the greenhouse effect is significant for our gardens.

The atmosphere is made up of a combination of gasses, as well as liquid droplets and solid particles, which are known as aerosols (Figure 3). The largest two constituents are nitrogen and oxygen, which by volume make up over 99 percent of the atmosphere. The other gasses that make up the remaining percent are known as trace gasses, and include water vapor, carbon dioxide, methane, nitrous oxide, ozone, and others. While found in very small proportions, the characteristics of trace gasses make them extremely important. Some of these gasses, specifically water vapor, carbon dioxide, methane, and nitrous oxide, are greenhouse gasses, and they help to regulate the temperature of the Earth and keep it habitable for human life.

One of the most important things we've learned so far is that the energy that heats the Earth and its atmosphere comes from the sun. The Earth is also emitting radiation on a regular basis, although of a much lower intensity than the sun. However, the atmospheric greenhouse effect doesn't work exactly like a traditional greenhouse.

Greenhouse gasses are selective absorbers of radiation: they preferentially absorb outgoing Earth radiation (infrared, or longwave), while they allow much of the sun's incoming (shortwave) radiation to pass through directly to the surface of the Earth. Thus, a portion of the radiation that the Earth emits is absorbed by greenhouse gasses and re-radiated back down to the Earth's surface. This acts like a blanket, keeping the Earth much warmer than it would be if there were no greenhouse gasses in the atmosphere. Simply put, the sun heats the ground, the ground heats the atmosphere.

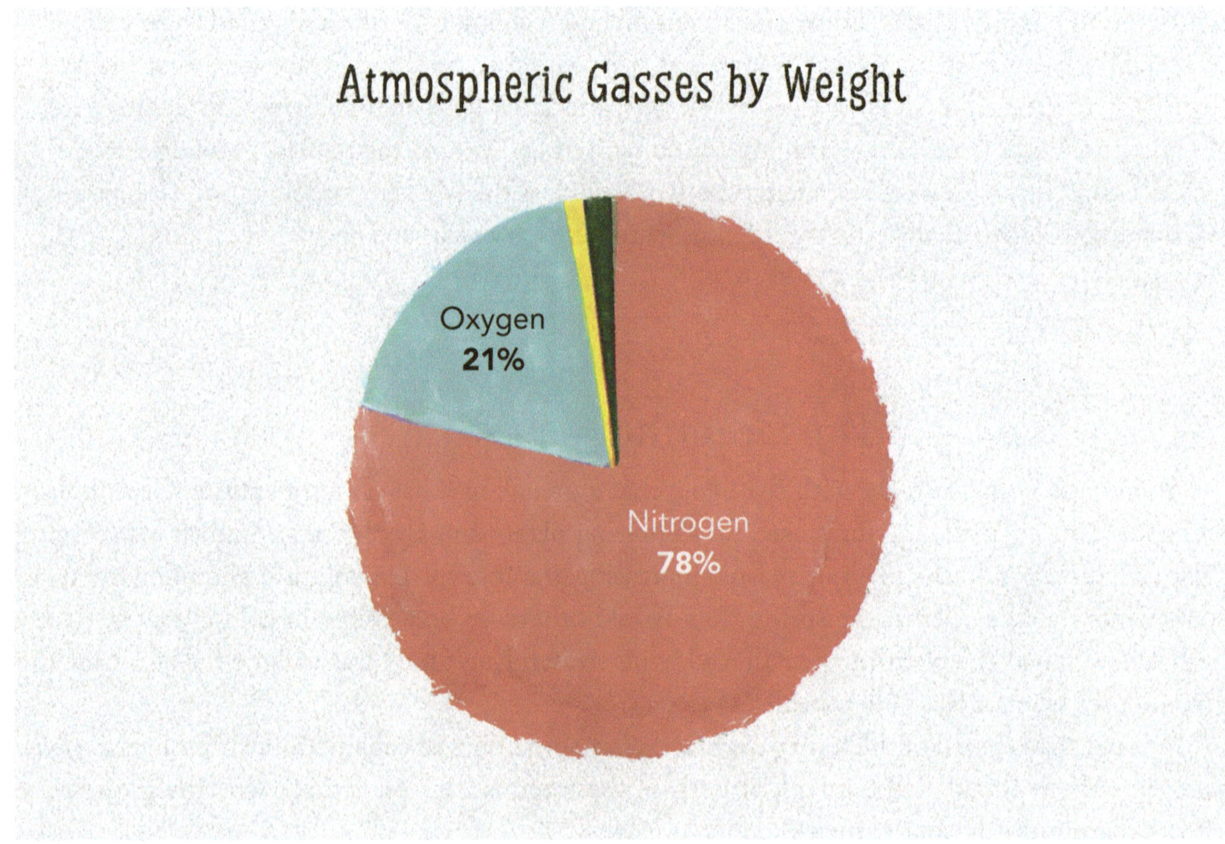

Figure 3

The greenhouse effect is even further enhanced when cloud cover is present. Cloud droplets, like greenhouse gasses, are selective absorbers, so clouds re-radiate outgoing Earth radiation back down to the surface. Thus, cloudy nights tend to be warmer than clear nights, all other factors being equal. If persistent cloud cover is present overnight, it can sometimes prevent the air from cooling so much that frost forms on sensitive plant leaves, allowing gardeners to breathe a sigh of relief.

Winter Topic #3: Why Is the Sky Blue?

This is often the first meteorology question asked by children—my younger self included! If you are outside in your garden, or perhaps inside at your desk working, but wishing you were outside, you have doubtless noticed that the sky can take on countless shades and colors. Let's dig a little deeper then, and instead ask, "What is it that makes the sky's appearance change?" (Photo 2)

While the optics of what we perceive with our eyes is a fascinating area of science itself, and one I am by no means an expert in, part of what our eyes see as sky color can be explained by atmospheric phenomena, specifically scattering. When we think of radiation coming in from the sun, it is important to remember that *all* types of energy, or wavelengths, of radiation are coming

Photo 2: The many cloud types, colors, and moods of the sky in upstate New York (all photos by author).

in. This includes X-rays and gamma rays on the shortwave (high-energy) end of the spectrum, all the way to TV and radio waves on the longwave end of the spectrum.

All types of radiation, ranging from long radio waves to very short X-ray and gamma rays, can carry energy through the vacuum of space. The length of these waves varies and falls on the electromagnetic (EM) spectrum (Figure 4). Visible light represents the portion of the EM spectrum we humans can perceive with our eyes. Red is the longest of those wavelengths, and violet is the shortest. Just outside the visible range beyond the red wavelengths is infrared radiation, which we feel as heat but cannot see. On the short end of the spectrum, just beyond violet light is ultraviolet light, which also cannot be seen by the human eye. Most of the energy that is emitted by the sun is in the form of visible light, or wavelengths that can be perceived by the human eye. Visible light has a shorter, and more intense, wavelength than infrared radiation, which is largely what the Earth emits and what we perceive as heat.

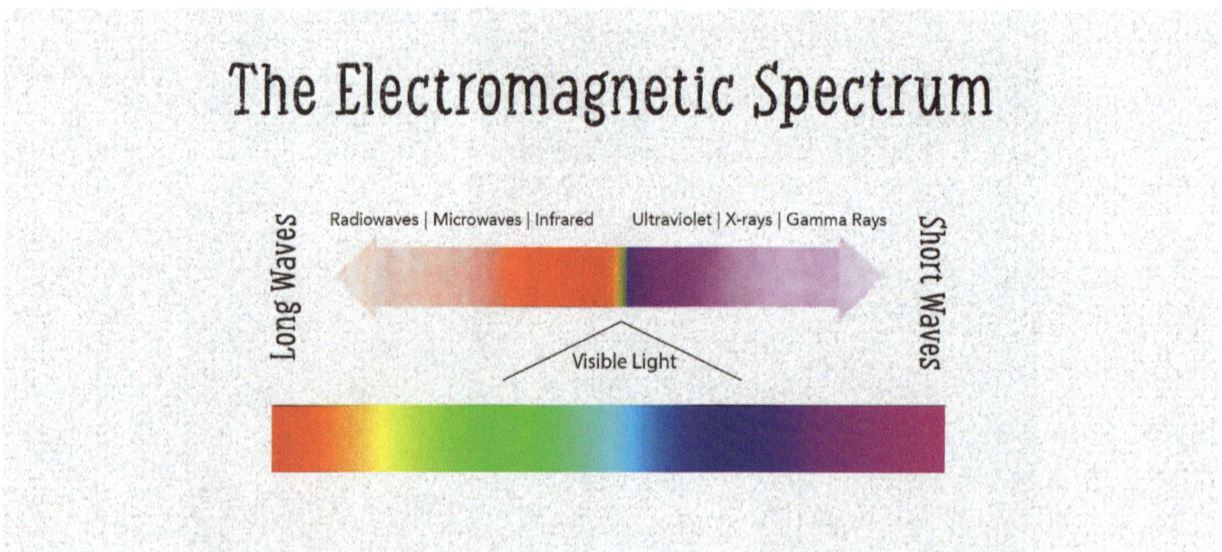

Figure 4

What happens to the mostly visible radiation that comes to us from the sun varies upon arrival. The radiation may be *reflected*. Just like a mirror, surfaces such as the top of thick clouds can prevent that radiation from ever reaching the Earth's surface by reflecting it directly back out to space. For this reason, cloudy days tend to be colder than clear days, all other factors being equal. Sometimes, the Earth's surface itself will reflect radiation back out to space if the surface is highly reflective. This property is known as albedo, and surfaces such as freshly fallen snow and light-colored beach sand have relatively high albedo.

Of the radiation that is not reflected back out to space, two other possible scenarios can occur. One is *absorption*; the radiation is directly absorbed by either gasses in the atmosphere or at the Earth's surface, increasing the temperature of the molecules that absorb it. The other is *scattering*, and this process explains why we see the sky as various colors.

Take a close look at the sky at various times of day. The morning and evening sky, depending on cloud cover, can have numerous soft colors ranging from purple to pink to orange. One of my favorite things to do on my early morning walks is to watch the sun rise. There is something magical about watching the sky turn from pitch black to a dark blue, and gradually transform with lighter and lighter colors in the eastern sky as the sun slowly comes up over the horizon.

Likewise, at the end of the day, the western sky is often ablaze with different colors. There is a golf course near my house that faces to the west and has some steep elevation increases. Standing at the top of the golf course in summer to watch the sun sink across the Hudson River to the west is phenomenal.

After observing and watching how the sky changes colors, you will likely notice that the "blue" sky can actually range from blue to a whitish shade. Scattering occurs as visible light enters the Earth's atmosphere and interacts with the gas molecules, or even tiny dust particles, and redirects the light coming in one direction into many directions. In one type of scattering, tiny gas molecules in the atmosphere preferentially scatter the wavelengths of light which are most similar in size to them—specifically blues, greens, and violets. The redirection of these wavelengths of light by atmospheric gasses is what gives the sky a bluish color to our eyes.

However, on those triple-H (hazy, hot, and humid) days of summer, you may notice that the sky is more of a white color rather than a brilliant blue. On these days, pollutants and other particles are trapped in a layer near the surface. These tiny particles are much larger than the gas

Figure 5

molecules which preferentially scatter blue and violet wavelengths of light. As a result, they scatter all wavelengths of visible light, and our eye perceives this as white light. Similarly, clouds appear white because cloud droplets also scatter all wavelengths of light efficiently.

At sunset, the sun is very low on the horizon and needs to pass through a much farther distance of the atmosphere to reach our eyes (Figure 5). The scattering of blues and violets by atmospheric gasses over a longer path length results in such a diffuse light that the blues and violets are no longer visible to our eyes. Longer wavelengths such as red and orange are not scattered as much, and thus pass through the atmosphere and reach our eyes.

As you can see, there are a multitude of reasons why the sky appears as it does on a particular day. Noticing and appreciating the colors as days and seasons change is something I will never tire of.

Winter Topic #4: Pressure and Wind

Perhaps the next most common weather question is "Why does the wind blow?" The winter, when those of us in northern climates are listening to the cold wind howl outside and dreaming of warmer days, is a great time to discuss this topic.

One of the simplest, and at the same time most difficult, lessons to learn when I first began studying meteorology is that the atmosphere is a three-dimensional fluid made up of four layers with varying temperature profiles (Figure 6). We all know the atmosphere has some depth to it, as planes can fly high up in the jet stream. What happens in the atmosphere above the surface can greatly affect what happens where we live at the ground, and vice versa. When you envision the atmosphere as a three-dimensional volume of molecules that are moving in space and time, you just begin to get a feeling for the level of complexity we're talking about.

In addition, atmospheric circulations are like fractals, geometric shapes that have similarities in structure at many scales. For example, rotational motions in the atmosphere can be as large as hurricanes, or as small as tiny dust devils. In this section, we will talk a little bit about how air moves in three dimensions.

The atmosphere is made up of many gas molecules which are "held," to some degree, near the Earth's surface due to gravity. The density of air (how many molecules there are in a given volume) is highest near the surface of the earth and decreases as altitude increases. This is why high-altitude mountain climbers need to acclimate for time periods: there is less air, and thus less oxygen, to inhale with every breath.

If we think for a moment about standing on the ground, the column of air molecules at any given time over our heads exerts a force. This force (per unit area) is what we call atmospheric pressure. Pressure, just like density, decreases with increasing altitude. While we don't usually notice the force of the air above our heads because we are acclimated to it, when there are rapid changes in pressure, our bodies definitely notice a difference. These changes can be felt in a variety of ways, such as ear popping, headaches, fatigue, and nausea.

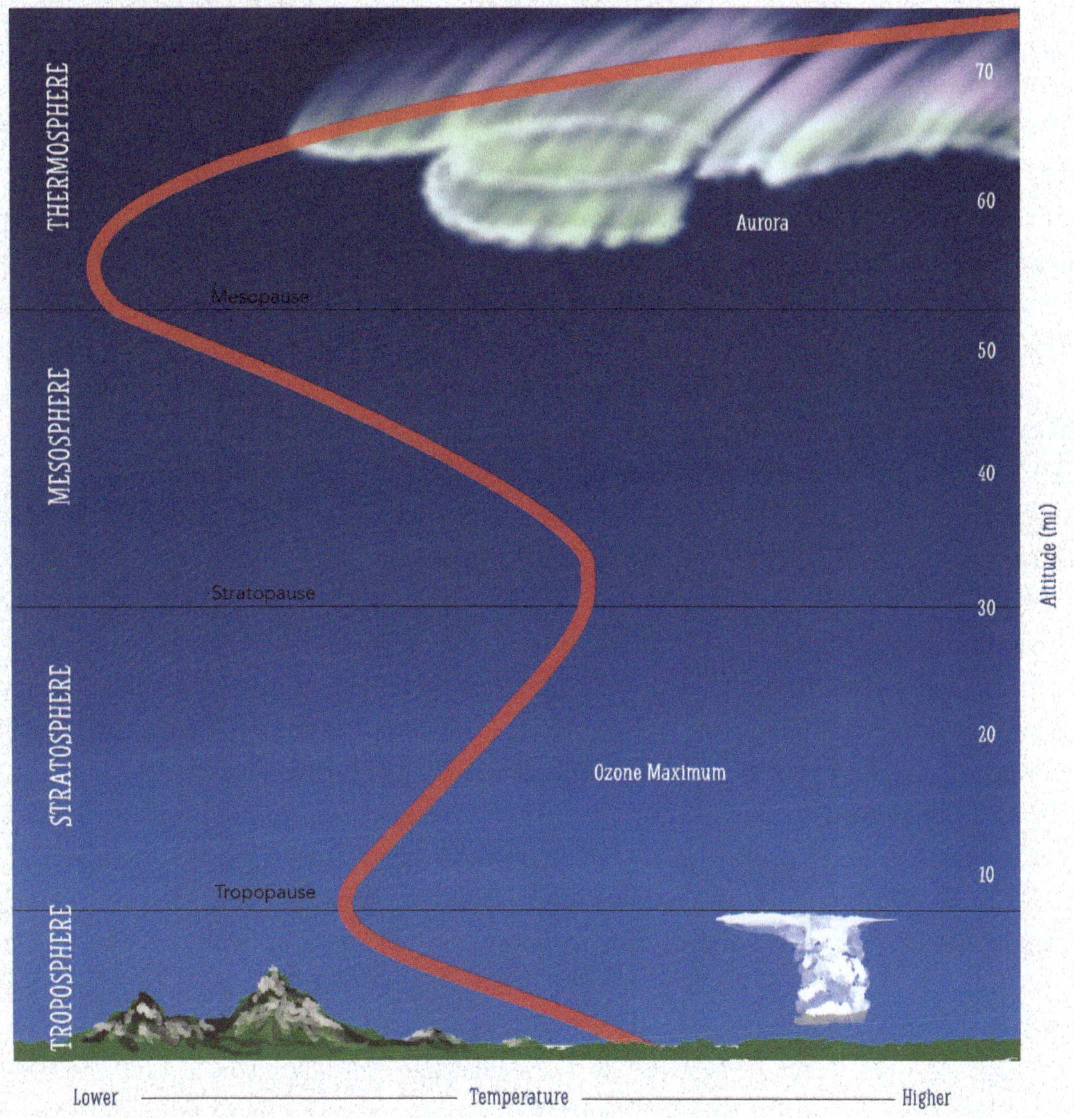

Figure 6

Even when our elevation does not change very much, motion within the atmosphere can cause areas of higher pressure and lower pressure. Many people experience physical symptoms, such as joint swelling, as weather patterns cause even small changes in air pressure. It is important here to note that vertical variations in air pressure, from the gravitational influence of Earth, are much larger than horizontal variations are.

All pressure variations, in all directions, are one of the primary reasons that air moves from place to place. Have you ever looked at a bathtub full of water? Imagine taking a board and swishing the water from one side to the other. You can actually force the water (briefly) to a position where there is more water on one side of the tub than the other. But then what happens? The water sloshes back from where there is more to where there is less to try to equalize itself. You can think of the atmosphere in a similar fashion: areas of high pressure are similar to the side of the bathtub where the water is deeper; low-pressure areas are analogous to where the water level is lower. Just like the water flows from high to low, so atmospheric molecules move from areas of high pressure to areas of low pressure. The pressure gradient, or the difference in the pressure from high to low, is what drives how fast air moves from place to place. This is wind, which is governed by the pressure gradient force.

There are many other forces that affect how the wind blows. Because the Earth is rotating on its axis and atmospheric molecules are not attached to the surface as we humans are, they experience what is known as the Coriolis effect. The Coriolis effect is an "apparent" force: it exists entirely because we are located on a moving (i.e., rotating) frame of reference.

When examined from the Earth, air motions in the Northern Hemisphere appear to be deflected to the right, while motions in the Southern Hemisphere are deflected to the left. Why is the deflection reversed in the Southern Hemisphere? Imagine looking at the North Pole from above.

Here, the sense of the Earth's rotation is counterclockwise. Now imagine looking at the South Pole from a similar perspective. The sense of the rotation is clockwise, in the opposite direction (this can be easily visualized by looking at a physical globe, or even a baseball, and watching it spin from the top and then from the bottom). Additionally, friction caused by movement of air over terrain, around buildings, and even between air molecules acts to slow the wind down. Friction is highest near the Earth's surface, where there are the most obstacles to airflow and where air density (concentration of air molecules) is highest, and decreases with altitude up to about 1.2 miles (2 kilometers). Above this level, friction is generally considered to be negligible.

Temperature variations can themselves cause horizontal variations in air pressure. Pressure goes down with increasing altitude everywhere, but it falls much faster for a given altitude change in a cold column of air. Correspondingly, pressure falls at a much slower rate in a warm column of air. These varied rates of change of pressure in the vertical can actually result in horizontal variations in pressure, and thus a pressure gradient force that will cause air to move from high to low pressure—wind. If you have ever felt a cool sea breeze off the water at the beach on a hot day, you have experienced this very phenomenon, known as a thermally driven circulation. Similarly, air tends to flow up mountain valleys during the day and down valley at night, when the air cools. These are known as valley breezes and mountain breezes, respectively.

Pressure is measured in units of millibars or inches of mercury. However, because pressure changes so much due to altitude alone, and mountainous areas have very large changes in elevation, it can be difficult to separate out variations in pressure due to weather systems from variations in pressure due to elevation changes. A correction factor is usually performed on pressure data that takes into account the station elevation, thus making it possible to compare pressure at stations of varying elevations and removing some of that elevation influence. However, "seeing" pressure variations on a weather map can still be very difficult, because there are hundreds of stations reporting pressure at any given time.

By connecting areas of uniform atmospheric pressure with lines, known as isobars, it is possible to visually digest the variations in a much easier way than it would be just trying to read numbers on a map. Isobars are usually drawn every four millibars. When the isobars are packed very close together, this indicates rapid pressure changes over short horizontal distances, or big pressure gradients. When the pressure gradient is weak, isobars tend to be spaced very far apart. So, it is possible to identify areas of fast wind speed on a map just by looking for areas where the isobars are closely spaced.

How do all of these forces work together to create movement of air, or wind? Believe it or not, we need to go back to basic principles of physics: Newton's second law, which states that:

Force = mass x acceleration

In other words, for any force that is exerted on the atmospheric molecules (pressure gradient force, Coriolis force, or friction, for example), there has to be a corresponding change in wind speed or direction (acceleration). The magnitude and direction of all these forces, and other, less important ones, are changing constantly in time and space. But air will always go to where the net, or cumulative, effect of where all these various forces are pushing. How fast it gets there depends on the strength of the force or push: bigger forces, higher wind speeds; smaller forces, lower wind speeds.

You might be thinking, "How does any of this relate to the weather that I, or my garden, experience at the surface?" Remember how we discussed earlier that the atmosphere is three-dimensional, and that there are interactions between the surface and the atmosphere, which extends high above the surface? At the surface, air circulations tend to be driven by three forces: pressure gradient force, Coriolis force, and friction. However, high up in the atmosphere, where we find the jet stream (which we will discuss in more detail later), friction is nearly zero, and thus air motions are primarily influenced by the other two forces. As a result, we tend to see patterns, called troughs and ridges, in the upper atmosphere, while at the surface we tend to see closed circulations around high and low pressure.

I will never forget one of the first times as an undergraduate that I felt I had really arrived at learning "real" meteorology. As an applied science, meteorology has a lot of core class requirements, including calculus, differential equations, physics, and chemistry. It is very easy to get bogged down in all the prerequisites and lose sight of what drove you into those classes in the first place. For me, the 'ah hah' moment was an introductory weather and forecasting class which I took during the spring semester of my sophomore year. In that class, we did a lot of hands-on work plotting weather maps, which was something I really enjoyed. Actually, looking at data on weather maps and figuring out what it means is still one of my favorite parts of the job today.

At any surface weather observing station, a multitude of parameters are recorded and reported every hour, if not more frequently. These often include temperature, dew point (a measure of humidity), wind speed, wind direction, present weather, barometric pressure, pressure tendency (is it rising or falling?), cloud cover, and many others. One of the things that makes meteorology such a complex science is the huge number of variables that must be considered. Even just plotting these variables on a map is quite an undertaking.

In order to be able to process the vast amount of data that existed even back in the "old days," before automated weather stations and computer models, it was necessary to form a convention by which the meteorological information could be displayed visually on a map and easily interpreted with the human eye. There were four key jobs that were necessary in order to make a weather forecast back in the early and mid-twentieth century: observers who would transmit weather data, plotters who would receive coded weather observations and plot them on a map, analysts who would draw contours and note the locations of fronts and high and low pressure systems, and forecasters, who would use these manually generated maps to actually create a weather forecast (10). As you can imagine, the process was exceedingly time consuming, and these skilled workers were in high demand as the number of weather stations and timing of observations increased exponentially.

Decoding Weather Station Models

Shown here is a sample of a surface map you might find online today. One of the first things you will notice is that there are numbers, colors, and symbols all over the map at each of the reporting stations. This information is plotted according to a convention known as the station model. The station models on this surface map are simplified, and contain some, but not all, of the information in the full model. On the map, the convention is as follows:

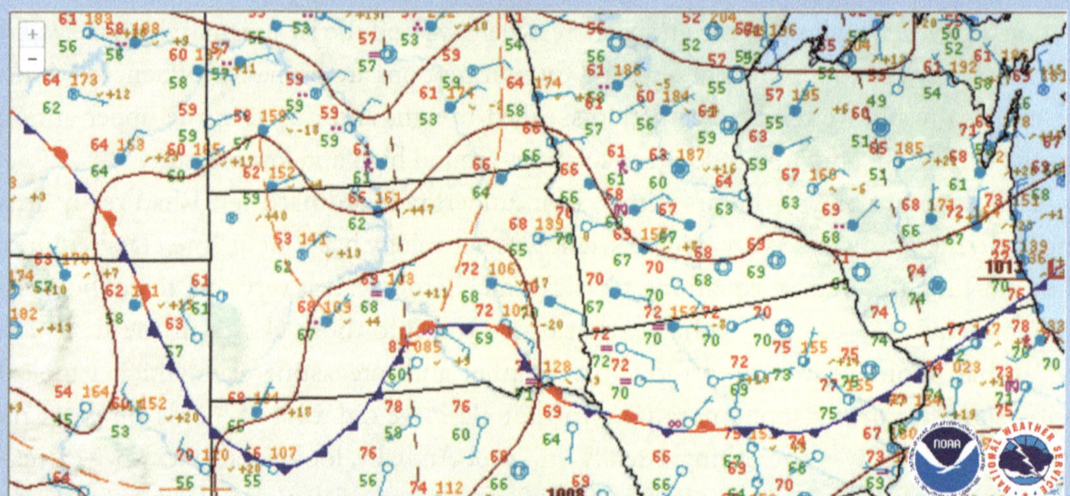

Figure 7

- The red number at the top left of each station plotted is the temperature.

- The green number at the bottom left is dew point.
- The shading of the circle on the map represents the observed cloud cover: the more of the circle that is filled in, the more cloud cover is present.
- The pink symbol in between the temperature and the dew point represents the observed present weather. Numerous symbols are used, including dots for rain, asterisks for snow, and one that looks like a lightning bolt for thunderstorms.
- The orange three-digit number on the top right represents the surface pressure, which is encoded so that it fits on the model as a three-digit number. Usually, pressures are in millibars and fall in the range of roughly 950 to 1050 millibars. Pressures are plotted to the tenths place and the leading 9 or 10 is omitted. Thus, 1031.0 mb would be encoded on the model as 310.
- Winds are shown with the "stick" pointing in the direction the wind is blowing from, with the flags representing the wind speed in knots or miles per hour (one short flag = 5, one long flag = 10, 1 pennant = 50).
- Indicators for high and low pressure centers ('H' and 'L'), isobars, and fronts may also be shown.

Plotting these parameters on surface maps allows meteorologists to identify key features and weather patterns. The data can be analyzed to further help with visualization, and important features such as locations of high- and low-pressure systems, fronts and other important features can be placed on the map.

Figure 8 shows a map of winds and isobars near the top of the jet stream, high in the troposphere (the lowest five miles of the atmosphere), where winds are moving from west to east largely parallel to the isobars. Note the wavy pattern to the airflow, where in some areas the air is moving in a counterclockwise direction, while in others the air is moving clockwise. Regions of cyclonic (or counterclockwise, in the Northern Hemisphere) air motion at this level are known as troughs, and areas of anticyclonic (or clockwise, in the Northern Hemisphere) motion are called ridges.

Now let's compare that to a surface map. At the surface, rather than waves, we see closed patterns of isobars around high- and low-pressure areas (also known as cyclones). Airflow is still cyclonic (counterclockwise) around the low and clockwise around the high, but rather than airflow being parallel to the isobars, there is a component across the isobars. Thus, the air is spiraling in toward the center of the low and spiraling away from the center of the high.

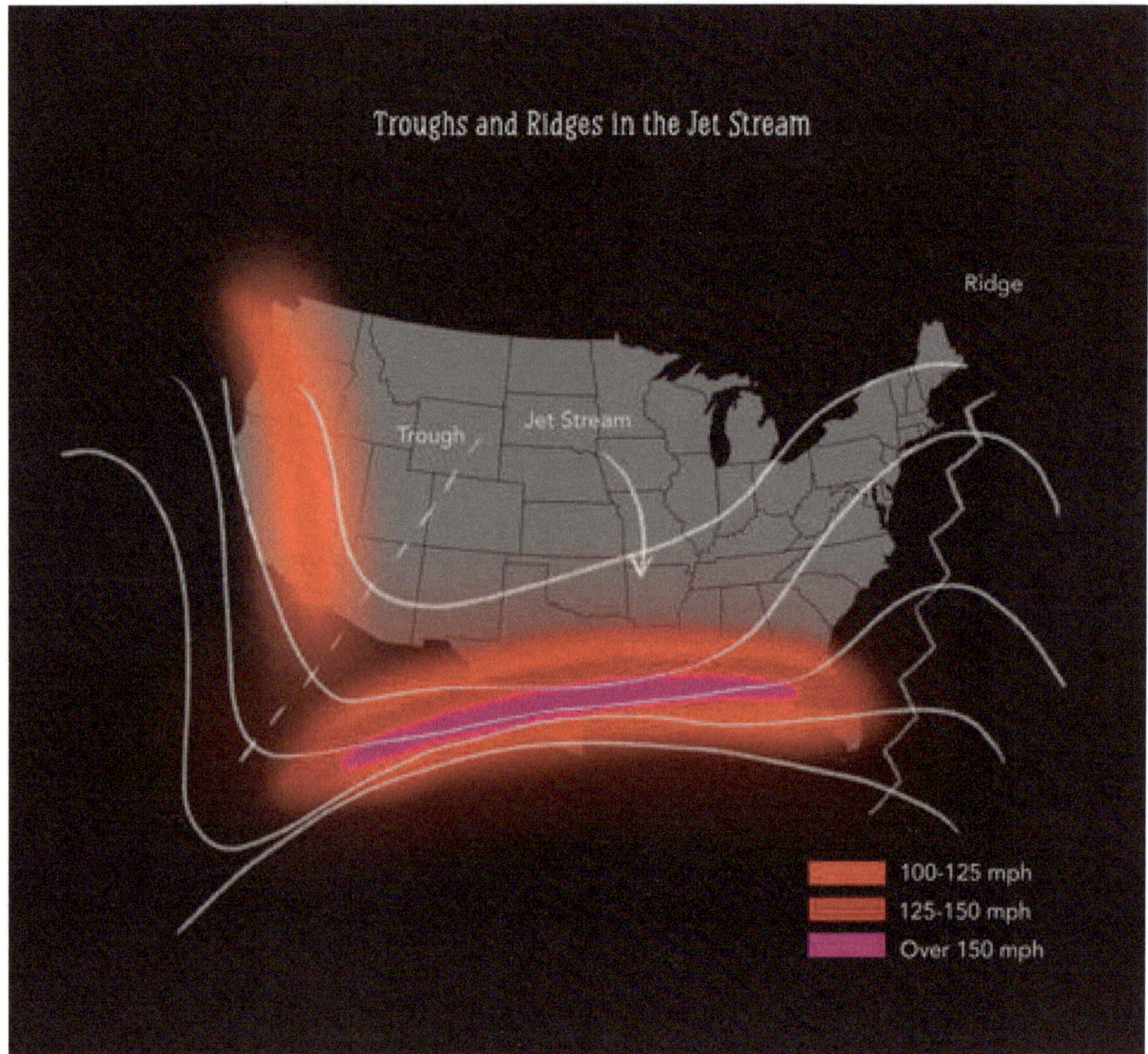

Figure 8

Finally, let's put it all together in three dimensions. Low pressure at the surface is created when an upper-level trough creates *divergence*, or spreading out, of air aloft. By "removing" air from a column at high levels, air pressure in the column decreases, and low pressure is born. Conversely, when air *converges* at high levels of the atmosphere, it is like adding air to a bicycle tire. Pressure of the column increases, creating high pressure.

Divergence tends to be greatest just ahead (downstream) of upper-level troughs, and convergence tends to be greatest downstream of upper-level ridges. Thus, the movement of upper-level air patterns is key to forecasting where surface highs and lows will form, how strong they will become, and how long they will last (Figure 9). Surface high pressure areas tend to bring clear, calm conditions and fair weather, while surface low pressures usually bring stormy conditions.

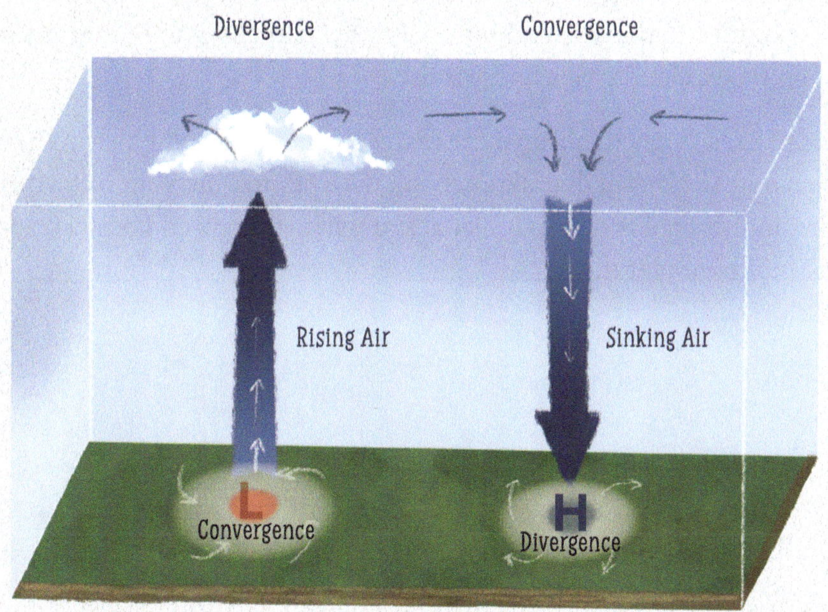

Figure 9

Wrap-up: Winter

In this chapter, we've just begun to dig in—pun intended!—to how the atmosphere works. Winter for gardeners is a time for waiting and planning and reflection. Winter is where the foundation is laid for all of those plans that come to life as soon as spring arrives. Similarly, we have laid the basic foundation here so that we can really understand how the atmosphere works and why we experience such varied weather from season to season and year to year.

In the next chapter, we will take a closer look at some of the more nuanced weather changes you may observe if you have been watching the weather at your location over long periods of time.

Gardener Goals

- Start tracking sunrise, sunset, shadow locations, and solar intensity (how strong the sun's rays feel) about once per week. Keep your notes in a simple notebook, and review about once every three months to become familiar with the sun's patterns where you live.
- Print out or view a daily surface map showing high- and low-pressure systems (for example, wpc.ncep.noaa.gov/dailywxmap). Make notes about where the systems are relative to your location, and what kind of weather you observe: changes in temperature, precipitation types, cloud cover, and winds.
- Take some time each day to observe the many colors and cloud types in the sky. You can take written notes or keep a digital notebook with photos and your observations. As you read further in this book, you can look back at what you saw and better understand why the sky looked the way it did!

Chapter 2

Spring

Spring Gardening: A Time of Changes

After many years—I won't say exactly how many—of living in the Northeast United States, I can confirm that spring, meteorologically defined as the months of March, April, and May, is not my favorite season. This may sound shocking coming from a person who loves to garden. After all, spring is the season when the action begins! Seed starting, transplanting, perennials returning from the ground after a long, cold winter—all the things that mark the start of a new growing season happen in the spring.

Spring in the Northeast, however, also has some less enjoyable attributes. In fact, spring in much of the Northeast is affectionately known as mud season (11). The Green Mountain Club, which, among other activities, educates people about Vermont's hiking trails and mountains and helps maintain the state's Long Trail System, notes that mud season occurs because warming air temperatures cause the ground to thaw near the surface, but thawing occurs more slowly deep in the ground. Because the ground is frozen underneath, even as surface temperatures warm, rain or snow melt is prevented from penetrating deep into the ground. The water sits in the surface layer and creates mud.

In addition to the mud, weather conditions in the spring vary tremendously from week to week and year to year. For example, in March 2018, four storms brought accumulating snow to parts of the Eastern Seaboard and repeated arctic air masses brought continued cold temperatures to the region (12). Conversely, spring can have the appearance of summer in some years, when heat returns early, at times before spring leaf-out has occurred (13).

In fact, early-season heat waves can be exacerbated when they occur prior to the appearance of leaves on the trees. When there are no leaves on the trees (and hence no photosynthesis occurring, which requires energy from the sun), all of the sun's energy is poured into melting the snow, and then into "sensible heating" of the Earth's surface. As someone who looks forward to warm summer weather, spring can be an infuriating season of warm weather punctuated by periods of cold, rain, and even snow that remind us that winter does not give up without a fight.

The transition from winter to summer in the Northeast does not happen gradually or linearly, but rather in discrete jumps and oscillations between warm and cold weather. As I sit here writing this chapter in May, the temperatures are cold enough that I needed to run the heat this morning. Tomorrow the high temperature will exceed 90 degrees Fahrenheit. While the sun's energy input to the Earth increases smoothly during March through May, what the Earth does with that increased radiation and how it distributes it around the globe is highly variable. The onset of spring and transition to summer is not like this everywhere in the United States. In fact, some areas, such as the Southeast, generally experience a much quicker transition from winter chill to summer heat.

There are numerous ways to track the onset of spring, and the National Phenology Network (NPN) is one of my favorite sources to learn how spring is progressing from year to year. I first learned about this organization at a conference talk during a meeting of the American Meteorological Society. The NPN, similar to volunteer weather observer networks, collects observations from thousands of volunteers around the country, organizes that data, and creates useful and interesting graphics. They also provide important information for policy and decision makers in many areas, including agriculture and invasive species management. The NPN refers to phenology as nature's calendar, and observers track a plethora of seasonal markers in both plant and animal species. Parameters tracked can include blossom growth on various tree species, animal migration patterns, insect emergence, and fall colors and the dropping of leaves from maples and other trees (14).

Weather and Agriculture: Fruit Trees

Farmers all around the world are heavily dependent on weather for income, and thus must take steps to extend the growing season as long as possible and combat weather conditions that may threaten a productive harvest. In 2023, a spring freeze destroyed Georgia's peach crop and many other sensitive crops in the Southeast. In 2012, New York State apple growers lost an entire year's worth of apples when a late spring hard freeze killed all of the cold-sensitive blossoms that had emerged on trees. Despite techniques such as running wind machines to circulate the air, the extreme cold effectively ended an entire growing season for apples in one night. That year, when my son went on the annual nursery school field trip to the apple orchard (a common occurrence in New York, a state known for its apple production), there were no apples for the children to watch run through the cider machines or pick off the trees. This resulted in a gaggle of three- and four-year olds who instead played apple-themed games and received coloring pages and an apple-shaped souvenir cup to take home. I forever remain grateful to the cheerful orchard owners who, despite having no apples, made it a fun experience for my son's class with their enthusiasm and innovation. As a parent chaperone, I found it impactful to talk with the owners and workers about how the weather had changed their plan for the year.

I have always been a rather simple gardener, true to my Italian heritage and the culture described by Mary Menniti at the Italian Garden Project (3). I try to use what tools and equipment I have available during the growing season. I recognize that I am fortunate, as a hobby gardener, that I am not reliant on my produce to feed my family or earn my livelihood. If I lose plants to animals, unfavorable weather, or, more frequently, to "operator error," I am generally able to compensate by buying a few new plants from the local nursery to replace them. I can simply watch the weather patterns to decide when to sow seeds in trays inside, when to sow early outdoor seeds, and when to move transplants from their happy spot in my sunroom-turned-office into the raised beds outdoors. Years of keeping a garden journal and taking weather observations on my property act as my own very simplistic version of the NPN, and allow me to observe patterns, year-to-year variability, and changes in how the growing season progresses from the onset of spring to my own little harvest (Photo 3). Let's go into a little more detail about how I personally track and observe the weather as I garden in each season.

Markers of the Onset of Spring

There are many markers of the onset of spring: the days get longer, animals come out of hibernation, buds appear on the trees (and allergies are ramping up!), and eventually blooms of all types appear. Gardeners and farmers will be starting early crops such as lettuce and peas just as soon as the ground is soft enough to dig.

Did you know that just like weather observers, there are volunteer observers who keep track of all of the markers of seasonal changes each year as well? The National Phenology Network was established in 2007 to "collect, store and share phenology data and information". Graphics and maps are created using statistics which are generated from years of observations of various plant species which are most active during early spring.

What kinds of parameters are tracked from year to year? Well for plants, parameters include when new spring growth appears, when leaves change color, when buds and blooms appear, and when fruit or seed drop occurs. Changes in animal species can be observed as well. Metrics such as when various stages of development of insects (caterpillars, pupae, and butterfly stages, for example) appear, mating behavior, and migrations are all indicators of the change of seasons. These observations are also useful for tracking the migration of pests or invasive species, such as the emerald ash borer.

This data network is invaluable as scientists seek to understand the impact of changes in climate on species of plants and animals. The data is used in conjunction with meteorological observations to understand how species, and entire ecosystems, respond to long-term changes in temperature and precipitation. The NPN publishes reports, as well as peer-reviewed journal articles, to describe and understand observed changes. For example, bees and birds tend to arrive earlier than they did decades ago in upstate New York. Additionally, the world-famous cherry blossoms in Washington D.C. bloom, on average, 11 days earlier than they did in the 1970s. There are numerous resources, reports, and information about how you can become an observer and help contribute to this invaluable data source by keeping track of seasonal changes in your own area.

Photo 3: Some of my most loved, most often used garden tools are not the shiny new ones, but the hefty old ones on which the handles have become smooth due to years of use. A few of my favorites are shown here. Left to right: a shovel is useful for digging large holes for new shrubs or clearing out large areas; a metal stake which is specifically made for tying up tomato plants, an old wood baseboard used for the same purpose, along with twine; hedge trimmers, a must have for boxwoods; a rake; a cultivator (although I've never called it that!), which I use for digging trenches or rows in my raised beds; small hedge trimmers for more delicate pruning (green handles); a hand tiller (blue T-shaped handle) is great for loosening up soil which has compacted over the winter in my raised beds; small pruning shears (above tiller, also sometimes known as bypass pruners) are used for pruning individual branches from shrubs; a small hand cultivator is useful for loosening soil in small areas; a hand trowel is one of my most often used tools- I use it for digging holes to transplant plants as well as for potted plants; large loppers provide great leverage for pruning branches bigger than about an inch in diameter; a good hoe with a sharp blade can be used for weeding and loosening soil. Far right: one of the most sentimental tools I own is my mother-in-law's pitchfork, which is excellent for digging larger stones and rocks out of soil, turning over compost piles, and working garden soil in raised beds.

March, the first month of meteorological spring, is generally when I start my seeds indoors. Although there is a great deal of variability on when I begin this task, it generally aligns more with my own schedule and I begin this task when I can find a free weekend, rather than any notable change in the weather. I have started indoor seeds as early as mid-March and as late as early April. It is always important to read the directions on seed packets, because every type of seed requires a different length of time to germinate and grow large enough to harden off and transplant. Additionally, knowing your average last frost date is helpful, as this is when you count backwards from in order to determine when to start your seeds indoors. Although it is possible to estimate when to start seeds indoors using the average last frost date, when I choose to plant my first outdoor seeds—carrots, lettuce, and peas—is heavily dependent on weather conditions in that given year. The most common time is late March or into the first few weeks of April. I usually look for cues such as the disappearance of most of the snowpack, the availability of compost at my local garden center, and a series of warm(ish) days that signal that the soil in my raised beds has thawed enough to dig.

If I plant directly into the ground, it may take even longer for the ground to thaw enough to work, but raised beds help mitigate this. I first mix up the soil and work some compost into each bed, just to ensure that there is healthy soil to start. Even in my small garden space, I still rotate my crops from year to year, and do not plant the same vegetables in the same beds each time. The cold-loving plants I sow directly outside are very low-maintenance: it is really just a "fix it and forget it" situation. Inevitably, cold weather and/or snow returns for a time after I sow the seeds, but every year they come up through the cold ground without fail.

The Dust Bowl

The 1930s in the central United States was characterized by persistent dry conditions, similar to the persistent multiyear drought that plagued much of the Western United States in recent years. The Great Plains and Midwest received much-below-normal rainfall in multiple years during the 1930s, and the winds that are so common in this flat area of the country caused blowing dust, hence the moniker Dust Bowl (15). While weather conditions over the decade set the stage for the misery of the Dust Bowl years, poor farming practices also caused problems. For example, improper crop rotation left the soil depleted of nutrients and susceptible to erosion by winds (16). Heat and insect pests also damaged crops. The social impacts of this agricultural downturn, as well as the larger economic downturn of the era known as the Great Depression, were wide-reaching (17) (18).

Many meteorology students choose to major in this field because of some impactful or exciting weather event they learned about or personally experienced, such as winter storms, hurricanes, or tornadoes. Very few students enter the field because they are interested in studying drought. However, drought has the potential to create widespread social and economic impacts over a long-term period. Thus, understanding the meteorological factors that come together to create and exacerbate drought conditions is extremely important.

Generally, drought conditions are defined by comparing current precipitation to normal levels on a weekly basis. Drought conditions can take several weeks to diagnose, or, in the case of a flash drought, occur suddenly. In either case, lack of rainfall in combination with abnormally high temperatures are often the primary driving factors. The U.S. Drought Monitor assesses conditions across the country and issues weekly updates on dry and drought conditions (19). Locations are rated on a scale ranging from D0 (abnormally dry) to D4 (exceptional drought).

Once these conditions are present, feedback can occur that makes conditions even worse. For example, dry soil does not absorb water well. When rainfall does occur, the much-needed precipitation tends to run off rather than being absorbed. By regularly tracking drought conditions where you live, you can adjust your watering schedule to changing conditions and ensure your garden is receiving adequate water even if rainfall has been lacking.

My indoor seeds, sown in seed trays, are a different story. I have found these to be much more finicky. My plant choices vary annually, but I usually sow some tomatoes, peppers, beans, and occasionally trial plants such as broccoli or eggplant indoors. Despite having a very sunny, warm room where I keep the trays, I have spent years trying to figure out why my plants sometimes grow leggy—tall and spindly, with few healthy, large leaves—or come up only to wither away, or don't come up at all. A couple things I've been able to narrow down over years of trial and error, which you may find helpful if you are starting seeds indoors:

1) Seed trays are very easy to overwater, and I have lost many new sprouts to mold due to overwatering. One tip I have learned is to insert a finger into the soil to about your first knuckle; if you can feel dampness, you may not need to water just yet.

2) Even in a room with ample natural light, spring in the Northeast just does not provide enough light for new seedlings, and so they grow leggy and tall as they strive to reach the sun's rays. This past year, I invested in a grow lamp which I ran for several hours per day to supplement the natural light coming in through the window, and I found I had much more success and healthier plants.

The next trial-and-error part of my gardening process also occurs in the spring, and it involves deciding when to move my new baby plants from their cozy interior room into the harsh outdoors. There are many ways to muck up this process, especially when one is starting off with weak seedlings. New plants need to be "hardened off" before being transplanted in their permanent outdoor home in the garden. This involves moving the trays outside for increasing periods of time over several days, to gradually acclimate the plants to the much-wider range of outdoor conditions than what they are used to inside.

During this process, I have lost plants to heat, too much direct sunlight, rain, and cold. I've found that healthier plants started under the grow light made for a much easier hardening-off period than in previous years. As a scientist, I know that there are other variables at play here, as well. For example, this past spring was relatively cool, but we didn't experience any major swings in temperature or excessive rain during the time period when I was hardening off my seedlings. It is important to pay close attention to weather conditions during the hardening-off period. Intense periods of direct sun, even if the air temperature is not too warm, can bleach the leaves of delicate plants. I find it helpful to put the plants outside in the morning, when it is still cool, and then watch the weather closely to decide when to bring them inside. Believe it or not, I have lost more seedlings due to intense sunshine than I have due to cold nights. Whatever the case may be for you, patience pays off: properly hardening off seedlings can take a few weeks, depending on the weather in any given year. Rushing the process only produces disappointing results, but careful monitoring produces hearty plants that thrive in the garden all summer long.

The final step in my spring vegetable garden is sowing my herb seeds. Sometimes these are seeds I have saved from the previous year, but sometimes I will supplement with a new packet or two. I keep herbs on my patio in pots for easy access when I am cooking; they also look lovely when they begin to grow! Similar to the cold-season crops, such as lettuce and peas, which I sow first thing in the spring, the herbs are fairly low-maintenance. I generally sow them later, to ensure that there is no danger of frost or snow once they sprout. The seeds are often tiny, and so simply raking them with a hand rake into the top layer of soil in the pot and watering gently is all that is needed. While it is often tempting to go to the garden center and pick up some of the large, leafy herbs in the six-pack trays that are already growing vigorously, the frugal gardener in me knows that I am only behind by a couple of weeks, and saving a lot of money by starting my own seeds saved from past years.

In addition to starting my vegetables and herbs, I also take inventory of my flowers and shrubs in the spring. I eagerly wait to see what plants come up, and what, if any, did not make it over the winter. Harsh winters in the Northeast can impact even cold-hardy plants, and I have lost more than one plant because the salt needed to make nearby walking surfaces safe can make its way to the plants and kill them. One of the most difficult things I have learned over the years is never to become too attached to plants. It is particularly difficult to part with the plants which were given to me by a friend or relative in commemoration of an event or loss.

The flower beds surrounding my house have many varieties of plants that come up at different times during the spring. Over the years of observing the onset of spring in my location, I have learned the rhythm of which plants wake up at which times. Watching spring unfold in this way is gratifying; just as I find myself with more energy as the weather warms and the days lengthen, the plants all around my yard respond in a similar way. Most of my shrubs are eaten down to twigs every winter by the very hungry and brazen deer which frequent our neighborhood, making everything look completely dead even as the weather warms. I have to be patient, because most years, almost everything comes back.

The forsythia bushes are first to sprout new leaves, which sport yellow flowers early in the spring and give the first breath of color to the garden. Not far behind are the azalea bushes and rhododendrons—I have some in the front of my house, where it's sunny and the plants bloom early, and some in the shady back area which bloom almost two weeks later. Last year, I noticed that the rhododendrons were looking dead in parts, so I unceremoniously chopped off anything that didn't appear to be producing. Lo and behold, this year the plants look much healthier and bloomed beautifully!

Next up are the ninebark shrubs, which produce dark purplish leaves, and shasta daisies (my favorites!), which grow vigorously with little maintenance. They come up early, and by June or early July I have heaps of cheery white and yellow flowers all around my house. In the shady part of my property around back, bleeding hearts are the early bloomers, and grow with abandon in May. Later, peonies, hydrangea, astilbe, and coral bells peek through the soil, and flower later in summer.

Rose bushes usually bloom later, as well. I have never considered myself a lover of roses, but I found a tiny one in a hidden part of my garden bed shortly after we moved in several years ago. I transplanted it to a more prominent place near my front door, and later added two other varieties to keep it company. They have taken off, and by July or so, produce beautiful roses that greet visitors as they round the corner to my front door.

The last plants to come out of winter hibernation are hibiscus and rose of Sharon (20). These two plants are "cousins," so their behavior is similar. The rose of Sharon bush on my property was there when we moved in, and my father and mother gifted me my first hibiscus in 2020. The dinner-plate-sized flowers on the hibiscus were bright spots in a very difficult year, so I bought one more hibiscus to place on the other side of the same garden bed where my first one was planted.

Every single year, without fail, I think these plants have died. Typically, one waits until the new growth appears from the bottom to cut back the dead branches from the previous year, and so these plants look dead for all the neighborhood to see, even into late May. Then, just when I am losing all hope, I see tiny new growth emerging from the bottom of the hibiscus. Once that pops up, I joyfully cut back all of the old dead branches and watch the new growth take off.

Other plants I have around my property, such as yarrow, phlox, and coneflowers, poke through in the spring and produce many flowers during the summer.

Spring in the Northeast, with its fickle weather, difficult growing conditions, and new growth can be a time of ups and downs for gardeners. Particularly for hobby gardeners like me, trial and error and study/observation over the course of many years gradually leads to the experience of knowing what works and what doesn't. With that in mind, let's move on to the weather section of this chapter, where we will discuss some topics that are highly relevant to backyard gardeners: temperature cycles, different types (scales) of weather systems, and some of the ways by which measurements of the atmosphere are taken.

Spring Topic #1: Daily and Seasonal Temperature Cycles

One of the reasons I enjoy gardening as a meteorologist is because it gives me a chance to be observant of the cycles that occur in nature over the course of a year. Not only is it a great way to find a rhythm in life, but it also is interesting to observe in nature some of the concepts I learned in school and now apply in my work. In Chapter 1, we talked about how it is the movement of the Earth in space relative to the sun that gives us our days/nights and seasons. Now we will zoom in a little bit more and look at some of the regional and local factors that can affect how temperature varies at a particular location.

One of the most prominent reasons for varying global temperatures is that the sun's radiation is more direct near the equator, and less direct near the poles. Thus, latitude, or north/south distance from the equator, is the primary factor that determines the general pattern of temperature of a place (Figure 10). Over the course of a year, areas which are close to the equator are receiving direct, or nearly direct, sunlight most of the time (think of that vertical flashlight beam, with its narrow, intense beam of light). Conversely, areas near the poles receive less intense radiation (think of the nearly horizontal flashlight beam with the weak light spread over a larger area) for some of the year, and even little to no incoming sunlight at times. With such weak radiation, temperatures at polar locations are

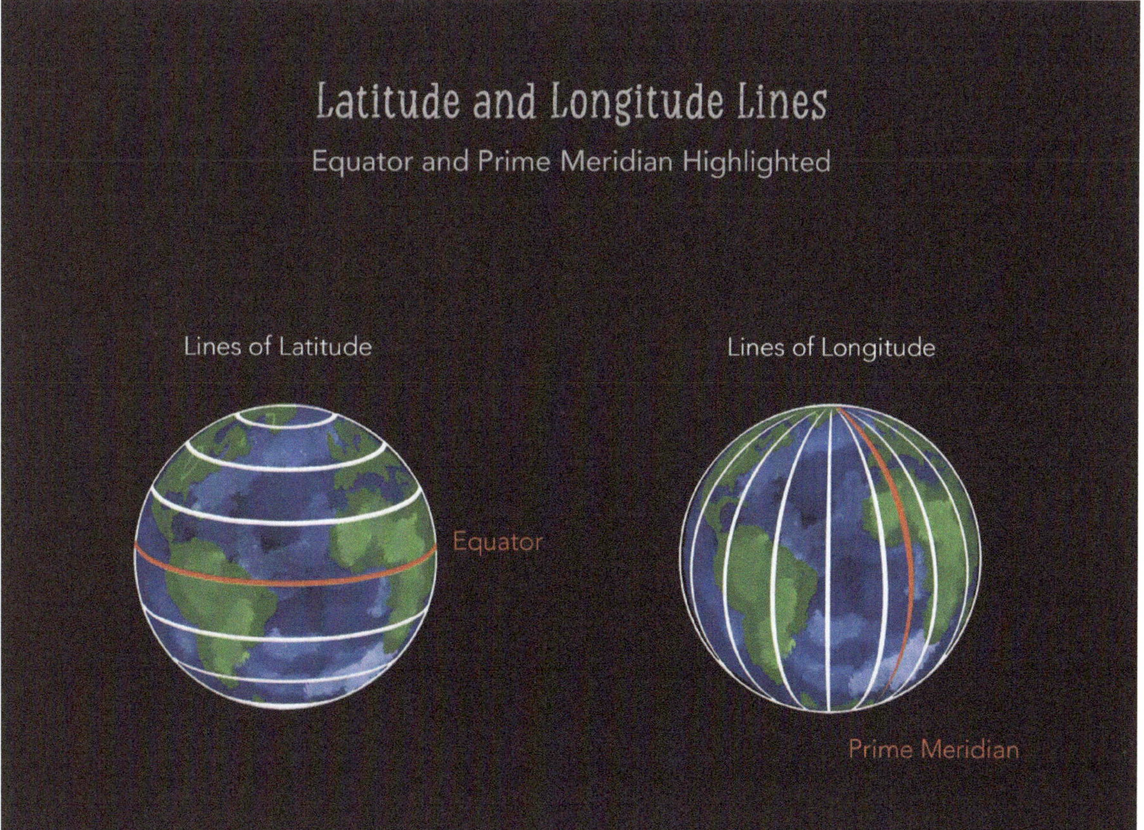

Figure 10

much colder overall. The primary reason that we have atmospheric circulations and ocean currents—which we will discuss later—is that the atmosphere and oceans are constantly trying to equalize the temperature imbalance that results from this differential heating between the equator and the poles.

Anyone who has lived in or visited a mountainous region or a city near a large ocean or body of water immediately knows that explaining temperature variations isn't quite so simple as I describe above. While latitude is the primary influence on temperature, there are many other factors that can cause regional and local variations.

Altitude, or elevation above sea level, also affects temperature. To illustrate this idea, let's look at two stations at relatively similar latitudes. Denver, Colorado is located at a latitude 39.8 degrees north of the equator and is at an elevation of 5,280 feet above sea level (a mile is 5,280 feet, which is why Denver is called the Mile High City!) Leadville, Colorado, only about 127 miles from Denver and at 39.2 degrees north latitude, holds the title of the highest-elevation city in the country, at 10,157 feet above sea level. The daily average temperature in January in Denver is 31.7 degrees Fahrenheit, while in Leadville the average temperature in January is a much colder 17.1 degrees Fahrenheit. Similarly, July average temperatures are about 20 degrees warmer in the lower-elevation Denver than they are in Leadville, where the average July temperature is only 55 degrees! These two cities are in close enough proximity that they would experience similar weather systems over the course of a year, and are at similar latitudes. However, the reason these two sites

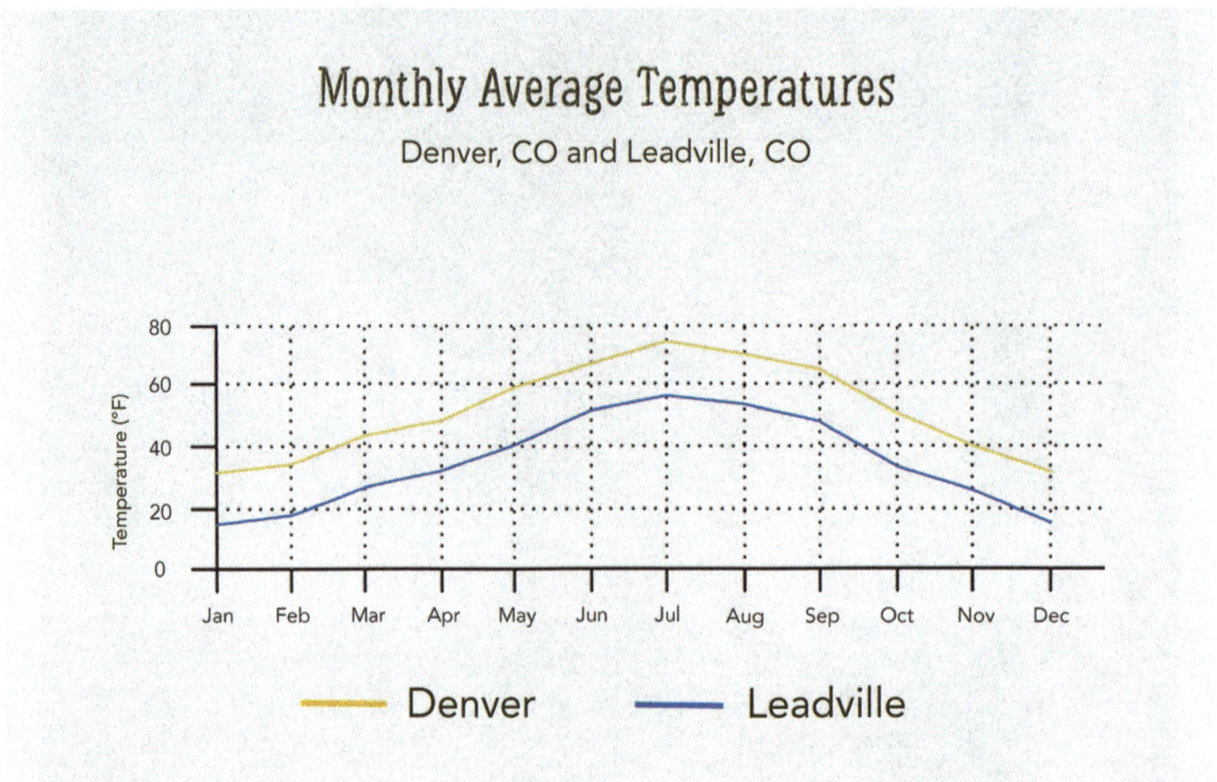

Figure 11

have such different temperature ranges over the course of a year is because Leadville is nearly 5,000 feet higher in elevation (Figure 11).

Another important factor that controls the temperature of a place is its proximity to large bodies of water. All other factors being equal, marine climates (cities near oceans, for example), are generally characterized by fewer extremes in temperature than locations that are in the middle of a large land mass. This is because of *specific heat*. Simply, this is a measure of the energy required to raise the temperature of a substance by a certain amount. Water has a much higher specific heat than land, which means that it requires much more energy to heat up water than to heat up land by the same amount. Conversely, water retains that heat much longer than land, meaning that water bodies tend to heat up slower and cool down slower than land. Anyone who has been to the beach has experienced specific heat: in the middle of the day, the sand can be so hot that it is nearly impossible to walk on it barefoot, while the water remains at a much colder temperature.

To visualize this effect, let's consider two United States cities at similar latitudes, but this time one will be in the middle of the continental United States, while the other is near an ocean: Bismarck, North Dakota (latitude 46.7 degrees north) and Seattle, Washington (latitude 47.4 degrees north). While Bismarck is 1,500 feet higher in elevation than Seattle, it is not near any oceans. Seattle, by contrast, sits very close to the coast in the Pacific Northwest. Over the course of the year, daily average temperatures in Bismarck range from 12.8 degrees Fahrenheit to 71.3 degrees Fahrenheit, while the temperatures in Seattle range from 42.8 degrees Fahrenheit to 67.1 degrees (21). Thus, Bismarck experiences a wider range of temperatures annually than Seattle because it is strongly influenced by land, which has a much lower specific heat than water. Seattle's climate is largely influenced by the Pacific Ocean, and experiences much smaller temperature ranges over the course of a year.

It is worth noting that extremes of temperature can and do occur at *all* locations, given the right meteorological conditions. It is possible for Seattle to receive snow on occasion; the city actually averages 6.3 inches of snow each year! Conversely, it is also possible for extreme heat to occur in a marine climate like Seattle's, such as when the heat wave in June 2021 sent temperatures soaring to over 100 degrees. We will delve a little deeper into the difference between weather and climate shortly. In this section we are primarily focusing on climate, or what most people would describe as typical conditions in a certain area.

The Seattle Heat Wave of 2021

In June and early July 2021, a record-breaking heat wave impacted the Pacific Northwest. Between June 26 and July 2, there were at least a hundred heat-related deaths in Washington State. The average high temperatures in Seattle in June and July are usually 69 and 72 degrees Fahrenheit. In Portland, Oregon, the average high temperatures in June and

July are 73 and 80 degrees Fahrenheit. During the heat wave, both Seattle and Portland, Oregon, recorded temperatures over 100 degrees for three consecutive days. The reported high temperature of 120 degrees Fahrenheit at Hanford, Washington on June 29 set a state record; Oregon set a state record-high temperature of 119 degrees Fahrenheit the same day. During the heat wave, British Columbia, Canada recorded an all-time high temperature of 121.3 degrees Fahrenheit.

The extreme temperatures across the region occurred as a result of an exceptionally strong ridge of high pressure aloft, which was located over western Canada. This ridge caused an unprecedented area of hot air to develop over the Pacific Northwest. Additionally, the system forced persistent offshore flow, allowing the hot continental air to spill westward even to coastal cities like Seattle, while keeping the cooler marine air offshore.

Subsequently, heat waves in the Northwest occurred in both 2022 and 2023. These events were less extreme than the 2021 event, but still brought abnormally warm temperatures to Washington. While it is important to note that specific weather patterns must occur in order for heat waves to occur in this region, when these episodes do happen, they occur in a warmer baseline environment than in the last century. Annual average air temperatures have risen by nearly two degrees Fahrenheit since 1900 in both Washington and Idaho, and by 2.5 degrees Fahrenheit in Oregon (22).

Let's now look a little closer at ocean currents, and rather than compare them to land, we'll compare them to each other. The oceans, due to their enormous volume of water, are the largest sink, or storage repository, for incoming solar radiation. Just like over land, equatorial waters receive more direct solar radiation and thus are much warmer than polar water. Unlike land, however, water is a fluid and able to move heat around by way of *convection* (a topic we will cover in more detail later, since convection also occurs in the atmosphere).

Essentially, warmer ocean waters move poleward via ocean currents, while cold waters move equatorward, trying to equalize the heating imbalance. Ocean currents thus serve the same purpose as atmospheric currents, but move on a much slower time scale than atmospheric circulations. Due to the Earth's rotation, ocean currents tend to move in a clockwise direction in the Northern Hemisphere, and counterclockwise in the Southern Hemisphere. In other words, ocean water moves from east to west near the equator, south to north along the east coasts of continents such as North America and Asia, west to east in the northern oceans, and then from north to south on the west side of continents (Figure 12). As a result, poleward-moving currents, such as the Gulf Stream along the Eastern Seaboard of the United States and the Kuroshio current in the Western Pacific, are much warmer than, for example, the California current on the West Coast of the United States. These ocean currents have a dramatic effect on temperature, and help to explain why the coastal waters at beaches all up and down the California coast are so much colder than beaches along the East Coast. Additionally, temperatures at coastal cities along the West Coast tend to be correspondingly colder than cities at similar latitudes on the East Coast.

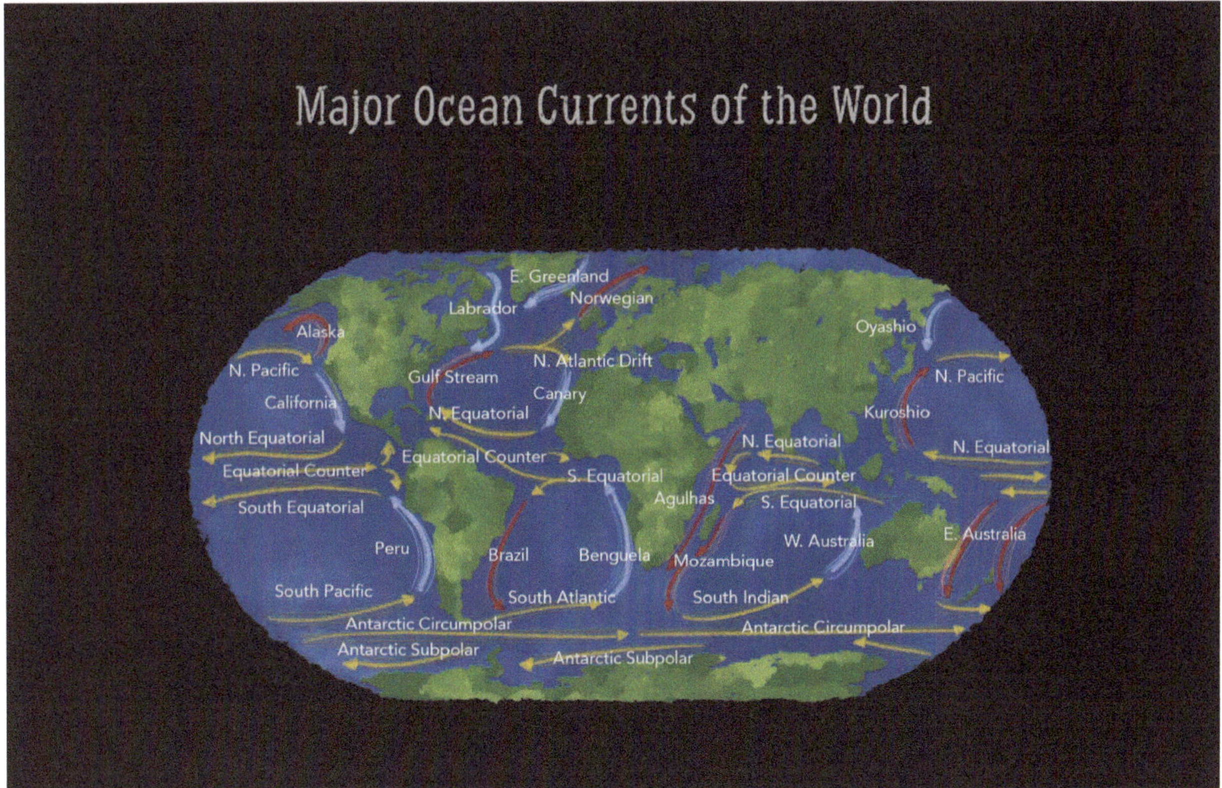

Figure 12

We have just covered a few of the large-scale controls of temperature that govern the climate of specific locations: latitude, elevation, land versus water, and ocean currents. Because there are so many other factors that contribute to small-scale, even local, climate effects, scientists use a fairly complex system of climate classification. Named after its developer, Wladimir Köppen, the Köppen classification system divides climates into five major types: tropical moist, dry, moist midlatitude with mild winters, moist midlatitude with severe winters, and polar. From there, climates are classified into subcategories based on seasonal patterns of temperature and precipitation. For example, upstate New York, where my garden is located, is generally classified as moist midlatitude, with long, cool summers and severe winters (Dfb).

As any upstate New York resident knows, "long, cool summers and severe winters" is an oversimplification. The same could be said for every other location, and brings us quite nicely into a discussion of weather versus climate.

As the saying goes, "Climate is what you expect; weather is what you get." The climate of a place is described by average conditions (such as what the Köppen system is based on) and extremes, or records. Both parameters are necessary to fully capture what really can be expected in a location.

For example, Phoenix, Arizona, and New Orleans, Louisiana, have similar monthly average temperatures in January and February. However, no one would characterize these two cities—one in the Southwest and one on the Gulf Coast—as having a similar climate. The extremes in Phoenix, particularly in terms of the highest high temperatures observed in January and February, are much greater than those in New Orleans.

The difference between climate, as characterized by averages and extremes, and weather is that weather is defined as the state of the atmosphere *at a specific time and place.* Weather simply describes what is going on when you look out the window, and it may or may not fit nicely into the climate classification as described by the Köppen system. However, repeated weather systems over time affect the average conditions and produce extremes (records), making weather and climate closely intertwined. We will spend the better part of this book discussing weather and the reasons why weather systems form and move the way they do, but the study of climate is a topic that could take up another whole book.

Spring Topic #2: Measuring the Atmosphere: Surface and Upper Air

As long as civilizations have existed, humans have observed the world around them. Initially, observations of storms and other weather events were recorded in descriptive language because instruments, and even a basic understanding that the atmosphere is an invisible combination of gasses, did not yet exist (Photo 4). By the 1600s, the first elementary instruments for measuring atmospheric parameters were developed. As technology and scientific knowledge continued to advance, better, cheaper, and more precise instruments followed. Today, instruments to measure the atmosphere are ground-based, remote from space, and everywhere in between. In this section, we will take a closer look at some of the parameters and instruments that meteorologists rely on to forecast and analyze the atmosphere (23).

Winds

Leon Battista Alberti is credited with inventing the first anemometer in the mid-1400s. His device was designed to measure wind speed and direction. Others, such as Robert Hooke, are also credited with later inventing the same device. Most mechanical anemometers operate on a principle similar to a child's pinwheel. Orient the device into the direction of the wind, and the rate of the spin is proportional to the wind speed: the anemometer spins faster as wind speed increases.

Today, mechanical anemometers are generally cup anemometers or aerovanes (Photo 5). Cup anemometers have three cups (about the size of golf balls sliced in half) mounted on a vertical pole. Airflow around the device causes the cups to spin, and they are calibrated to measure wind speed

Observations on the weather
Philadelphia 1776

July.	hour.	thermom.
1.	9-0 A.M.	81½
	7- P.M	82.
2.	6. A.M.	78.
	9-40' A.M.	78
	9. P.M.	74
3.	5-30' A.M.	71½
	1-30. P.M.	76
	8-10.	74.
4.	6. A.M.	68.
	9.	72¼
	1. P.M.	76
	9.	73½
5.	6. A.M.	71½
	9.	72
	9. P.M.	74.
6.	5. A.M.	74.
	9.	75.
	4. P.M.	77.
	10.	74.
7.	6. A.M.	71.
	10.	73.
	1. P.M.	74.
	3-20'.	75
	9-30.	74
8.	5-35' Am	75
	9.	77½
	2. P.M.	80.
	5.	81.
	8-15'	80
	9-30	79

day	h. m.	°
9	5-30 A.M.	75
	9	77½
	6-30 P.M.	81½
	9-45	78.
10.	8. A.M.	75.
	9-15.	76½
	2-0. P.M.	80.
	4-45'	82.
	6-30	81½
	9-30.	78.
11.	5-30. A.M.	74.
	8.	76½
	9-40. P.M.	75.
12.	7. a.m.	72.
	9.	72.
	8-50. P.m.	72.
13.	5-30. a.m.	71½
	11.	74
	2. P.m.	76
	6-45.	76
	7-25	76
	9-	75
	rain	
14.	6-50. a.m.	73.
	rain	
	9-30.	72
	rain.	
	1. P.	71½
	rain 5-35	70
	5. 8-35	

Photo 4: Thomas Jefferson's weather observations from July 1776. Image courtesy: jefferson-weather-records.org.

to an accuracy of plus or minus two knots (about 2.3 miles per hour). They are usually paired with a wind vane to measure wind direction. Aerovanes, or vane anemometers, combine the wind vane and the anemometer into a single device. The unit spins so it is oriented in the direction of the wind, and its propeller then spins in proportion to the rate of the wind speed.

Photo 5: Left: Anemometer and wind vane as part of a weather station. Image courtesy: MagicFoundry/Flickr. Right: The Robinson anemometer. Image courtesy: NOAA.

Other types of anemometers in use today operate on nonmechanical principles. For example, sonic anemometers measure wind speed by measuring changes in the speed of ultrasonic sound waves between two sensors. Although these units are not generally used in federally-maintained automated observation systems, many private industries use these types of devices for measuring the wind in places where having a device without moving parts (which can break) is a benefit—for example, where icy conditions cause anemometers with moving parts to freeze up. Sometimes these devices are used alongside traditional mechanical anemometers for comparison.

Winds are highly variable by nature, so an averaging period is used to smooth out chaotic variations in wind speed and direction. Standard weather-observing stations contain anemometers mounted at 10 meters (approximately 32 feet) above the ground, and average the wind over a two-minute time period. This is what is commonly known as sustained wind speed. In blustery conditions, wind gusts (how much the instantaneous wind exceeds the two-minute average) are reported as well. The reason for mounting anemometers so high above the ground is to avoid blockages due to trees, buildings, terrain and other obstacles. For this reason, it is also best to mount anemometers in open areas instead of near obstacles that may cause variations in wind speed or direction.

Pressure

In 1643 or 1644, Italian scientist Evangelista Torricelli conducted a series of experiments using mercury in a glass tube, essentially proving that the atmosphere has mass and inventing the first barometer to measure atmospheric pressure (24).

Torricelli filled a glass tube with mercury, then inverted the tube into a bowl of mercury, creating a vacuum in the tube. As air pressure pushing on the mercury in the bowl increased and decreased, the mercury was forced up and drawn down from the tube (Figure 13). Modern mercury barometers work on the same concept! Any fluid can be used to measure atmospheric pressure in this way, but mercury is generally the fluid of choice because of its high density.

Small changes in atmospheric pressure push mercury up and down a tube that is just under three feet tall, and the atmospheric pressure is recorded in inches of mercury, or in Hg. Technically speaking, the mass and weight of the air molecules are different things, and both of these are different from the atmospheric pressure, which is the force (per unit area, such as square foot) exerted

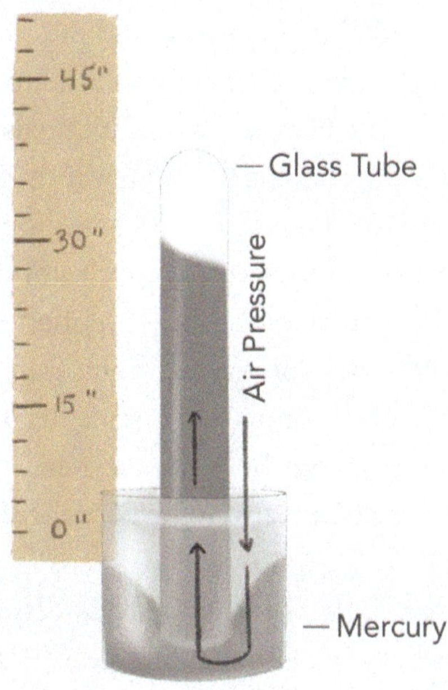

Figure 13

by the molecules of the atmosphere on us at the ground. Barometers measure these changes in atmospheric pressure. Today, modern atmospheric pressure sensors in automated weather stations use pressure transducers, or devices that convert measurements of atmospheric pressure into an electrical signal. Rather than using mercury, pressure changes are sensed by a diaphragm, and work similarly to how your ear drum flexes in response to changes in atmospheric pressure. These sensors are extremely accurate and can give nearly continuous readings of atmospheric pressure (25). At many automated sites, there are either two or three pressure sensors, and the sensor data from each is checked against the others to ensure readings are in agreement.

Temperature

In terms of weather instrumentation, the thermometer has nearly as long a history as the barometer. Although Galileo Galilei is often credited with inventing the first thermometer, the device he invented in 1596 is, in fact, called a thermoscope. This tool consisted of a water-filled glass with a long neck at the top. When the glass was immersed in hot water or otherwise heated, the fluid inside rose up the neck of the device. The thermoscope measured changes in the density of water due to variations in temperature, but not temperature itself (26).

In 1612, Santorio Santorio built on Galileo's earlier device by adding a measurement scale to it. This device later evolved into the thermometer we know today, and thus there is some contention over who was the actual inventor of the thermometer (27).

By the time of the Colonial Era in the United States, several devices for measuring temperature had become widely available and the practice of taking weather observations was much more common. Many of the founding fathers took daily weather observations and kept detailed records. Thomas Jefferson may be one of the best-known individuals of that era who took weather observations for many decades at Monticello, his home in Virginia (28).

Thermometers were often marked or graduated based on the phase change points of water, its melting point and the boiling point. However, the scales of degree increments were not standardized. In 1724, Daniel Fahrenheit, creator of the Fahrenheit scale, marked zero on his scale as the coldest point he could get a salt-water solution to reach (salt water freezes at a colder temperature than plain water), and fixed another point on his scale at 96 degrees, what he thought to be the average human body temperature. From here, he measured the boiling point of water to be 212 degrees and the freezing point of plain water to be 32 degrees. This scale is still commonly used in the United States today.

Swedish astronomer Anders Celsius developed his centigrade (now known as Celsius) scale in 1742 based on 100 degrees between the freezing point (at zero) and the boiling point (at 100) of pure water. This eventually became part of the metric system of measurements in which all units are based on a decimal, or base-10, system. The Celsius scale is used in the vast majority of countries around the world, with the United States being an obvious exception. The Celsius scale has the same scale as the scientific Kelvin scale, except that zero on the Kelvin scale is based upon the theoretical point at which all molecular motion ceases. In other words, the increment of one Kelvin degree is equivalent to one Celsius degree, except the zero point on the scale is shifted down by just over 273 degrees (29).

Today, there are several types of thermometers (Photo 6) which can be used to measure air temperature. Galileo thermometers are visually interesting; I actually have one as a functional decoration on my mantle! These glass cylinders are filled with a clear liquid and several small glass spheres containing liquids of varying densities. The liquids in each sphere are usually different colors and have a metal tag with a temperature imprinted on it. The spheres rise as the temperature cools and sink as the temperature warms. The air temperature is read by averaging the temperature indicator on the lowest floating sphere and the highest sphere at the bottom of the cylinder. Although Galileo thermometers are not particularly accurate, they are beautiful and make great conversation starters for discussing principles like temperature and density.

Photo 6: Left: Galileo thermometer. Top right: bimetal strip thermometer. Bottom right: standard automated temperature sensor inside ventilated shelter. Image courtesy: Famartin, under a CC-BY-SA 3.0 license.

Another common type of thermometer is the bi-metal strip thermometer. These are often found in simple garden thermometers available at any big-box store, as well as in kitchen thermometers and other places where inexpensive measuring tools are important. Two different metal strips are fused together, and they expand and contract differently as the air temperature changes. The amount of deformation in the strip can be calibrated to a scale that reads the temperature. However, they can be knocked out of calibration very easily should the device be dropped.

As is the case with pressure measurements, temperature measurements today are generally taken by automated sensors. Often, temperature is taken using a type of electrical resistor in which measured electrical resistance is calibrated directly to changes in temperature. These devices are accurate to within about plus or minus two degrees Fahrenheit (25). In federally maintained and operated automated sensors across the United States, 1-minute average and 5-minute average temperature are reported. The sensors are mounted at a standard height of two meters (approximately six feet) above the surface. Additionally, six-hour maximum and minimum temperatures are reported four times per day, and daily maximum and minimum temperatures are reported once daily at midnight. Data from these automated weather stations and human observers from earlier years can be used to look at long-term trends and changes in local temperature.

Humidity

Humidity, or the amount of water vapor in the atmosphere, is one of the more complex parameters to accurately measure. Water vapor is an invisible gas that makes up to about four percent of the weight of the atmosphere. Most of the water vapor content of the atmosphere is contained near the surface for two reasons: evaporation from the oceans is the primary source of water vapor in the atmosphere, and temperatures are so cold at high altitudes that very little vapor can be contained in that air.

Most basic meteorology textbooks include a whole chapter on atmospheric humidity, and these open with a discussion of two related topics: phase changes of water and saturation. Water is a unique substance because it can exist in all three phases at pressures and temperatures commonly observed at the Earth's surface. Ice, liquid water, and water vapor can all be present in the same area at the same time. Contrast this with, say, aluminum, which exists only in solid form at commonly observed temperatures and pressures. For aluminum to melt, it must be heated to 1,221 degrees Fahrenheit, and in order to create aluminum vapor, it would need to be heated to a whopping 4,478 degrees Fahrenheit!

Phase Changes of Water

When a substance exists in solid form, the strong bonds holding the molecules together are keeping that substance in a rigid, organized state–like an ice cube, which will hold its shape as long as it remains frozen. When a substance is heated to its melting point, enough energy is added to break some of the bonds holding the molecules together. There is still some loose connection, but a liquid will generally take the shape of whatever container it is put in rather than hold its own shape. When even more heat is added, the substance gains enough energy to break the bonds and release individual molecules into vapor. Although many people think of a whistling teakettle as an illustration of water vapor, this is incorrect, because what is coming out of the teakettle is steam, or condensed drops of liquid water. Water vapor is, by definition, invisible, so we cannot see it with the naked eye.

When water changes from one phase to another, you can clearly observe the direct link between heat, energy, and temperature. Imagine an ice cube in a pan on the stove, with the burner turned on. If we measured its temperature, that ice cube would gradually get warmer and warmer as the ice cube is heated. Heat—the transfer of thermal energy—would eventually bring the ice cube to its melting point at 32 degrees Fahrenheit. If the burner remained on, the temperature of the ice would no longer increase, because the energy would go into breaking molecular bonds, and the cube would start to melt. Once all of the ice melted into liquid water, the temperature would again begin to increase, until the water reached its boiling point of 212 degrees Fahrenheit. At that point, individual water molecules would gain enough energy to release themselves from the liquid, and evaporation would occur. The water would continue to boil, remaining at 212 degrees Fahrenheit, until all of it evaporated away.

When water changes phase from solid to liquid (melting) or liquid to gas (evaporation), energy needs to be added. When water changes phase in the reverse direction, from gas to liquid (condensation) or liquid to solid (freezing), that same amount of energy is released back into the atmosphere. It is even possible for water to completely bypass the liquid phase and go directly from solid to gas (sublimation) or gas to solid (deposition). It takes more energy to evaporate water than to melt it, and it takes the most energy to sublimate it. Conversely, the most energy is released when deposition occurs, and less so with condensation and freezing.

Although a glass of water appears to be static, if we could zoom in at a molecular level and take a close look at the surface of the water, we would see a lot of activity going on. At any given moment, individual molecules are leaving the liquid (evaporating), while other water vapor molecules in the atmosphere are hitting the surface and becoming liquid (condensing). When evaporation and condensation are occurring at the same rate, the level of the water in the glass remains constant. When evaporation is occurring faster than condensation, the level drops; think of a puddle evaporating after a summer rainstorm. When condensation occurs at a greater rate than evaporation, the water level will rise; think of the drops that form on your bathroom mirror when a hot shower is turned on.

Why all of this discussion about phase changes of water? It is very important to our discussion of humidity and humidity measurement. *Saturation* is defined as the point when both evaporation and condensation are occurring at the same rate; the level of the glass remains constant. As it turns out, the saturation point depends on the air temperature. In Chapter 1, we noted that the air feels much less humid in the winter than in the summer. This is because the saturation point of warm air, known as the saturation vapor pressure, is much higher than that of cold air. In other words, warm air has the capacity to hold a lot more water vapor than cold air, and a lot more evaporation can occur before that saturation point is reached than when the air is cold. Although supersaturated conditions are possible to obtain in a lab, in the atmosphere the air rarely goes far past the saturation point. When the air is *supersaturated*, or contains more water vapor than is allowed for that temperature, condensation occurs so that the water vapor is removed from the air and converted to liquid form. In your bathroom, supersaturation results in liquid drops forming on the surface of the mirror as water vapor is removed from the air. In the atmosphere, supersaturation results in the formation of clouds (above the surface), fog, or dew (at the surface).

Knowing where the air is relative to its saturation point, or the humidity, is crucial to understanding how and where clouds, and ultimately precipitation, will form. There is not a simple instrument, like an anemometer or thermometer, that we can use to measure humidity. Instead, there are several instruments and methods, each of which have pros and cons.

Most early hygrometers (devices that measure humidity) compared differences in the weight or characteristics of an item, such as the weight of a piece of charcoal or the length of a piece of hair, and related that to changes in atmospheric humidity. In the 1400s, Leonardo da Vinci invented a hygrometer made up of two balancing pans. One contained beeswax, which is waterproof, and the other contained cotton or other substances that attract water from the air. As the atmospheric humidity changed and the substance opposite the beeswax absorbed or released water, the slight differences in orientation of a horizontal stick between the two pans could be calibrated to measure humidity (30). Modern hygrometers often measure changes in electrical resistance or thermal conductivity to assess humidity.

Relative humidity is perhaps the most common parameter that the general public uses to assess humidity. Relative humidity is simply a percent value indicating how close the air is to its saturation point. One hundred percent relative humidity means the air is completely saturated. At 50 percent relative humidity, the air is halfway to its saturation point.

The problem with relative humidity is exactly as its name suggests: it is *relative* to the air temperature, and thus does not give a concrete measurement of exactly how much water vapor there is in the air. Air at 100 percent relative humidity at 75 degrees Fahrenheit contains far more water vapor than air at 100 percent relative humidity at 20 degrees Fahrenheit. In fact, relative humidity can vary throughout the day as the air temperature rises and drops, without the addition or subtraction of any water vapor to the air.

Another common measurement for humidity is the *dew point*. As we've discussed, relative humidity can change during the course of a day without any changes in water vapor content. As the air warms, its saturation point increases, and that air has the capacity to contain more water vapor than it did when it was cold. Thus, it moves farther away from the saturation point. Similarly, as air cools, it has less capacity to contain water vapor as its saturation point decreases, and the relative humidity increases. In other words, relative humidity and temperature vary *inversely* with each other. As one goes up, the other goes down, and vice versa. If the air is cooling, say, during the overnight hours, and its relative humidity increases to 100 percent, then the condition of saturation has been met and dew or fog will form. If the air temperature is below freezing, then frost may form on your garden plants and cause damage. In most federally maintained automated sensors, humidity is measured by way of a mirror that is cooled until dew or frost appears on the surface. The temperature (measured by the automated unit, as discussed above) at which this happens is the dew point temperature.

There are other parameters that assess water vapor content of the atmosphere, and which are used for mathematical calculations, but we will not discuss those in detail here. They include specific humidity, absolute humidity, and mixing ratio. Each of these has their uses in atmospheric science, but each also has drawbacks, and some are used with more regularity than others. Dew point is commonly used because it is one of the easiest parameters to measure; many of the other parameters, which are more useful mathematically, can be obtained from the dew point.

Automated Surface Observing Systems (ASOS)

While we have discussed some of the specific parameters that give us information about the state of the atmosphere, we have not yet addressed the importance of having this information at multiple places at many times of day. There are many automated observing networks in the United States and around the world. Here in the United States, one of the best-known and commonly used is the Automated Surface Observing Systems, or ASOS network. This is a collection of more than 900 automated weather observing stations across the United States, many of which are located at airports to support the Federal Aviation Administration (FAA) and aviation operations. The sensors were installed as a collaborative effort between the FAA, the National Weather Service, and the Department of Defense. These stations are built according to standardized siting parameters (such as 2-meter temperatures and 10-meter winds), and are operated and maintained by the government. The data they collect are input into computer models, along with other types of weather data, and are useful for forecasting. In addition, the data can be very useful for monitoring real-time weather conditions, as well as analyzing past weather events.

ASOS units monitor wind, pressure, temperature, and dew point using instrumentation we have already discussed. These units are equipped with instruments to measure many other parameters as well. Some of these include cloud cover (to be discussed in more detail in Chapter 3), visibility, present weather type, and liquid precipitation amounts. For all the economic benefits of having automated sensors rather than trained human observers, there are still some parameters that ASOS units are not able to report. Weather conditions such as hail, blowing dust or sand, and snowfall/snow depth all need to be reported by a human observer. Thus, at many ASOS sites there are trained weather observers who can adjust or supplement the automated observations when conditions warrant.

There are many other automated observing networks in addition to the federal ASOS network. Many states have mesoscale (smaller scale) networks, or *mesonets*. Some of these weather stations include additional information such as soil moisture and temperature, along with camera images that can help meteorologists identify ongoing weather conditions when there is not a human on the premises. Offshore, the United States operates an extensive network of buoys which also transmit weather conditions. These units are especially valuable when weather features, such as hurricanes, are approaching the coastline. Ships and planes are also equipped with weather-observing technology, and those observations can be transmitted to and archived by the federal government for the purposes of weather monitoring and study.

Radiosondes

We have discussed the many types of ground-based weather observations that can be taken right from the surface of the Earth. However, we previously learned that the atmosphere is not flat, but rather is a three-dimensional fluid that covers the surface of the Earth which is detectable up to over 300 miles above the Earth's surface. However, when one compares it to the size of the Earth itself, the depth of the atmosphere is tiny, like the skin of an orange, and most of the weather occurs in the lowest six miles or so. It is important to take measurements of wind, temperature, and moisture within that layer to better understand how air and weather systems move around the globe.

In order to accomplish this, the most common practice is to use radiosondes. Similar to the ASOS network, radiosonde stations are located all across the United States and around the world. Radiosonde technology was developed back in the 1930s. A weather instrument package, complete with electrical sensors, is launched via a helium or hydrogen balloon into the atmosphere at a prescribed time of day. On the East Coast of the United States, those times are 7:00 a.m. and 7:00 p.m. during Standard Time, and 8:00 a.m. and 8:00 p.m. during Daylight Time. On the West Coast, balloons are launched three hours earlier, 4:00 a.m. and 4:00 p.m. during Standard Time, and 5:00 a.m. and 5:00 p.m. during Daylight Time. Thus, the balloons are all being released in concurrence, providing a three-dimensional snapshot of the atmosphere twice daily.

The instrument package rises through the atmosphere, taking measurements as it goes. The inflated balloon gradually expands as it rises, eventually reaching the limits of the latex from which it is constructed. The balloon bursts, a parachute deploys, and the instrument package floats gently back to Earth. These packages are equipped with a self-addressed, postage-paid return envelope so that they can be returned to the federal government, refurbished, and reused. Approximately 20% of radiosondes are returned in this way (31).

The balloons are tracked by Global Positioning Satellite (GPS) technology. Many drift on air currents and land miles from the original launch site. On the East Coast, many of the balloons drift with the jet stream and land in the Atlantic Ocean!

Universal Coordinated Time

Universal Coordinated Time (UTC) was formerly known as Greenwich Mean Time (GMT). It is sometimes known as Zulu time (Z), which comes from the aviation field because the Prime Meridian is the zero meridian, and the call sign for the letter Z is Zulu. UTC, the somewhat confusing acronym that meteorologists use, came about as a sort of compromise between languages. In order to have one acronym across multiple languages, the International Telecommunication Union settled on a universal acronym.

UTC time is a standard by which all time zones are set. UTC time was set based on the time at the Prime Meridian in Greenwich, England, hence the occasionally used acronym GMT. However, UTC time does not change during the year, whereas the United Kingdom shifts to British Summer Time (BST) during the summer months, at the same time we in the United States shift to Daylight Saving Time. For this reason, the time in Greenwich, England, is not actually always the same as UTC time!

Where I live in the Eastern time zone, we are five hours behind UTC (UTC -5), except during Daylight Saving Time, when we are four hours behind UTC (UTC -4). On the West Coast during Standard Time, the clocks are eight hours behind UTC time (UTC -8); during Daylight Saving Time they are seven hours behind (UTC -7).

Displaying all weather graphics and maps in a singular time zone creates uniformity, and much easier interpretation by scientists in any time zone. Looking at a surface weather map with observations taken at 12Z, or 1200 UTC, we can see all observations taken at the same time, regardless of location or time of year. For example, in the United States, a 12Z map depicts weather conditions taken at 7:00 a.m. EST, 6:00 a.m. CST, 5:00 a.m. MST, and 4:00 a.m. PST. UTC time is based on a 24-hour clock, so there is additionally no confusion with a.m. and p.m. on maps. If a meteorologist is interested in observations from a particular location, it is very easy to convert from UTC time to local time.

There are many other, less commonly used methods to take direct measurements of the upper atmosphere. Sometimes when a hurricane is approaching the U.S. coastline, National Oceanic and Atmospheric Administration (NOAA) aircraft are deployed to take reconnaissance flights across the storm. These aircraft are equipped with measurement sensors, and deploy dropsondes—similar to radiosondes, but they fall down through the storm rather than rising upward. NOAA has partnered with the private company Saildrone to launch drones into hurricanes as another way to take measurements and better forecast these storms.

Remote Sensing

Up to this point, we have covered the various types of instruments that can take weather observations directly, either on the ground or above the surface. But there is also an invaluable set of resources known as remote sensing technology, which take measurements of the atmosphere at a place other than where the weather instrument is located. The two most common technologies, which we will discuss here, are radar and satellite.

Formation of the National Weather Service

While many people are aware of how important the National Weather Service (NWS) is in protecting lives and property, some may not be aware of the unique history of the agency, the role it has played in our nation's history, and how technological advances have helped to improve the science of weather forecasting by leaps and bounds over the past 150 years.

Many prominent and not-so-prominent individuals in our country's history, including the founding fathers, made a daily habit of taking weather observations, closely following and documenting local weather. By the turn of the nineteenth century, researchers understood that compiling regional weather observations and understanding larger-scale weather patterns could be useful in forecasting the weather. Volunteer weather observers have always been invaluable to scientists in taking field measurements and advancing our understanding of how the atmosphere works. In 1849, Joseph Henry, who was the first director of the Smithsonian Institute, developed a small network of trained volunteer weather observers who took observations of temperature, precipitation, and other weather parameters. Henry was one of the first to recommend the creation of a National Weather Service. Though many individuals in our country's history made a daily habit of taking weather observations, there was no centralized, concerted effort on the part of the U.S. government to issue forecasts or warnings until nearly 100 years into our nation's history.

In 1869, Wisconsin congressman Halbert E. Paine wrote a bill that created the National Weather Service under the domain of the U.S. Signal Service. On February 9, 1870, President Ulysses S. Grant signed a joint congressional resolution that formed the National Weather Service. In 1940, the National Weather Service was moved under the domain of the U.S. Department of Commerce, where it still resides today.

As the National Weather Service looks to the future, its focus is on creating a weather-ready nation in which communities and individuals are prepared and informed before and during inclement weather, and responsive and resilient after an event occurs. The focus is now not only on disseminating crucial weather information, forecasts, and warnings, but also in helping people understand how to receive and make appropriate decisions based upon that information. The National Weather Service continues to pursue partnerships with key agencies, companies, and individuals in support of its mission.

The satellite era is arguably one of the most important advances in weather observation and forecasting since the development of the original barometer, thermometer, and telegraph; the latter enabled immediate transmission of weather information over long distances. Prior to 1958, when the first weather satellite, named Explorer, was launched, it was not possible to see weather systems over the oceans unless some unlucky ship found itself caught in the path of a storm (32). Even then, there was no guarantee that the weather reports would make it back to shore in time to warn the public, if they made it back at all. The Galveston hurricane of 1900 is one of many tragic examples where a storm approached, largely unseen, until it was too late to evacuate the public. With the ability to see storms in their formative stages and track them across the Atlantic Ocean, it suddenly became possible to issue warnings so people could prepare and evacuate if necessary.

The Galveston Hurricane

A few years back, I read the book "Isaac's Storm" by Erik Larsen, about Isaac Cline and the 1900 Galveston, Texas hurricane; one of the deadliest in American history. Cline was the chief of the U.S. Weather Bureau (precursor to the National Weather Service) in Galveston, and initially believed that a hurricane could never do any harm to Galveston because "they recurve to the north and east in the Gulf of Mexico." His written opinion on the topic was actually used to prevent the construction of a seawall prior to the 1900 storm.

The book opens on September 7, 1900, the day before the storm, and gives a detailed narrative of events that day and those that followed. The story is told from Cline's perspective and is filled with his personal stories, as well as those of other residents.

The book includes a discussion of what is known about the evolution of the storm itself, from its origins in the eastern Atlantic Ocean to its eventual landfall on Galveston. The saga is constructed, when possible, from ship's records and other historical documents, and is told along with a layperson's discussion of how hurricanes form.

Perhaps the most interesting part for me, which built a foreboding sense of doom, was the story of the ship Louisiana, captained by T. P. Halsey, which sustained a direct hit as the storm was undergoing rapid intensification in the Gulf of Mexico. Captain Halsey estimated the winds to be 150 miles per hour. Larsen describes what may have been occurring on the ship as a result.

The storm surge from the Galveston Hurricane covered the island with several feet of water. As the tragedy unfolded, many individuals were left frantically scrambling for safety, despite the last-ditch efforts of Cline to issue a hurricane warning without waiting for prior approval from Washington, D.C. Although Cline later claimed to have warned people on the beach to seek higher ground, the author clearly believes he never did so.

An estimated 1,000 people lost their lives as a result of the Galveston Hurricane. Isaac Cline himself lost his pregnant wife, although he and his brother Joseph were able to save his three young daughters. The Galveston Hurricane remains one of the deadliest weather disasters in U.S. history. In 1902, the city constructed a seawall, which remains today and has protected the island numerous times, saving both property and lives.

Several types of satellites orbit the earth at different levels. The most common are Geostationary Operational Environmental Satellites, or GOES. These satellites, and others operated by other nations, orbit at approximately 22,000 miles above the Earth's surface. For comparison, GPS satellites fly at about 12,600 miles altitude, and commercial airplanes fly between six and eight miles above the Earth's surface. At this altitude, the satellite follows a spot on the surface, so the image the satellite "sees" remains stationary even as the Earth rotates on its axis (hence the term *geostationary*). One of the GOES satellites follows the eastern half of the United States; another follows the west. Other geostationary satellites around the world monitor different parts of the globe, and thus it is possible to "see" the entire Earth from space. Satellites do more than just take camera-style pictures of the Earth, although these are both useful and beautiful! The many instruments on board a satellite measure parameters such as outgoing radiation, water vapor, and even lightning. Although they are by far one of the most expensive weather observing technologies, they have become invaluable to the study of meteorology and have allowed for great advances in the quality of computer weather forecasts (see satellite images in Photo 7).

Polar Orbiting Satellites

Polar orbiting satellites orbit the Earth at 500 miles above the surface, a much lower altitude than geostationary satellites. These satellites don't fix on a single point, but rather circle the Earth in a path that crosses the poles. It takes just under two hours for a polar orbiting satellite to complete a full circle from North Pole to South Pole and back again.

Since they are so much nearer to the surface of the Earth, these satellites are able to zoom in much closer than geostationary satellites. Just like zooming in with a camera or on your phone, the closer vantage point allows for more close-up detail, but does not show the wider view. As the polar orbiting satellites circle above the Earth from pole to pole, the Earth is constantly rotating underneath them, once every 24 hours. The satellite eventually traverses a path that covers the entire globe over a period of about 14 hours, passing over each spot roughly twice per day.

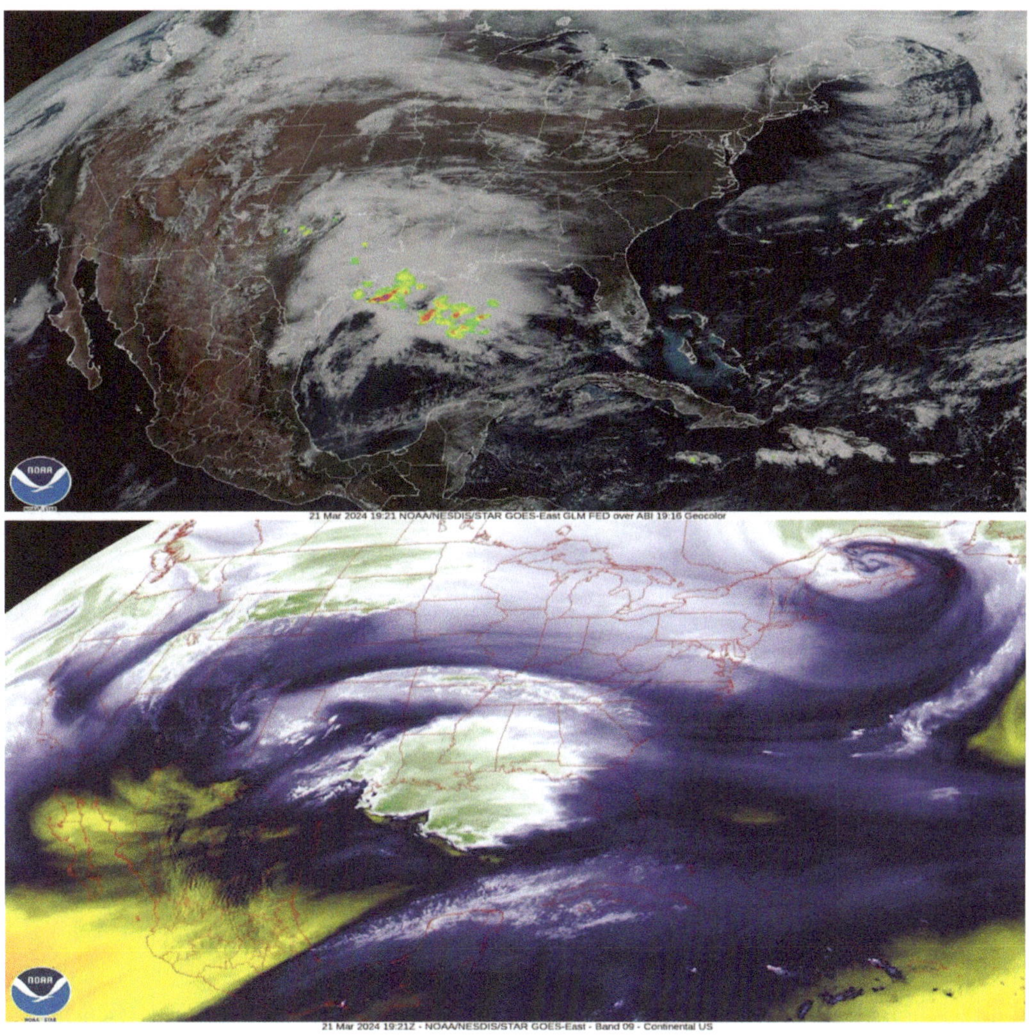

Photo 7: Top: NOAA geostationary satellite image showing visible imagery and lightning strikes. Intense thunderstorms are occurring in the Gulf of Mexico. Bottom: NOAA geostationary satellite image, from the same time as top image, showing upper-level water vapor.

Radar is another type of remote sensing equipment; unlike satellites that orbit the Earth, radar is ground-based. Radar operates by sending out a beam of microwave radiation. That beam bounces off of reflecting targets and returns a signal to the radar, which is known as reflectivity (Figure 14). Generally, the reflecting targets are precipitation particles (cloud droplets are too tiny), although radars have been known to pick up signals from bats, birds, and many other non-meteorological sources.

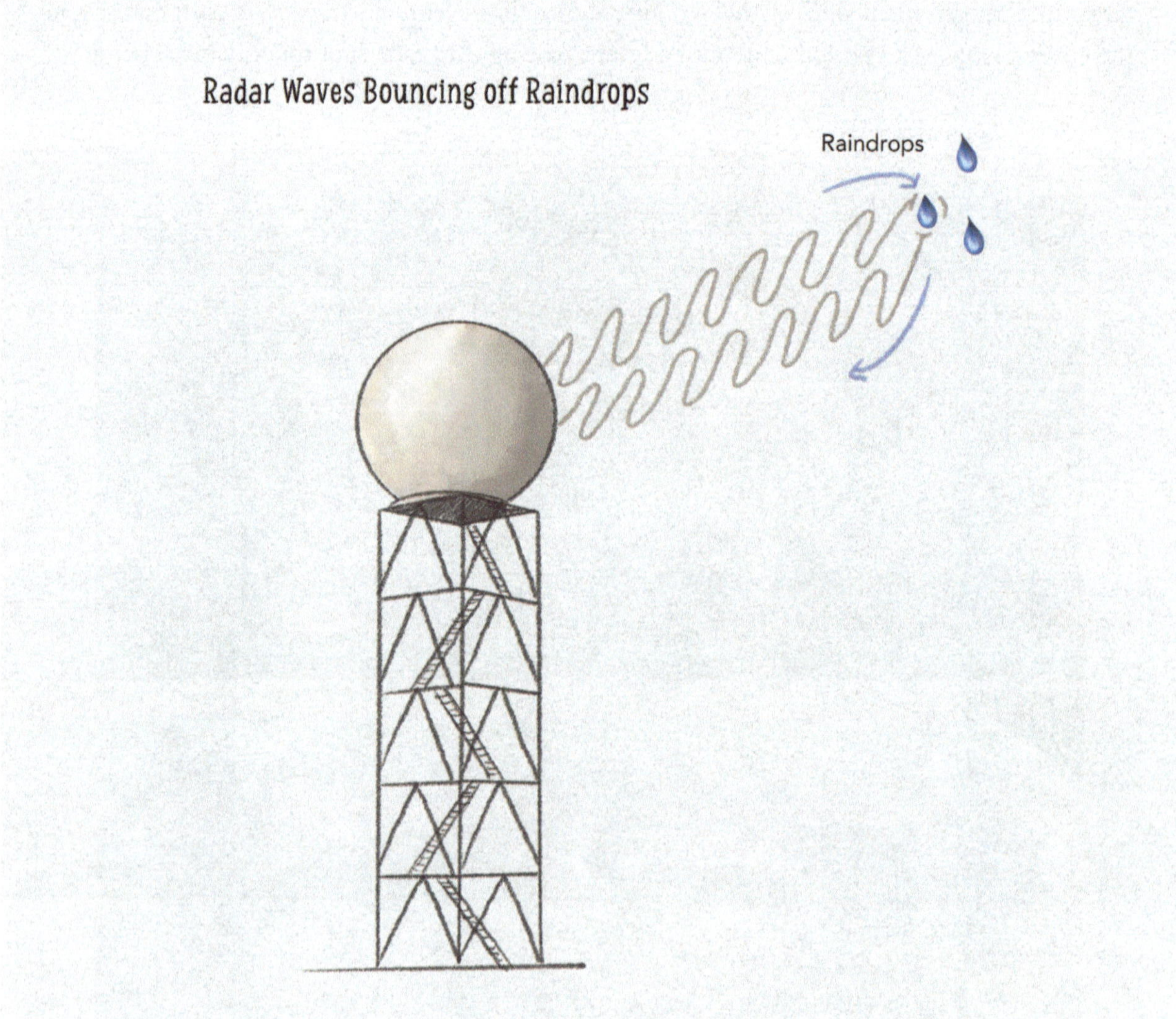

Figure 14

The radar beam is elevated above the ground, and as the unit spins around, it can create a circular picture about 500 miles in diameter of where the reflecting targets are (33). The units of reflectivity are decibels, or dBZ. Areas of high reflectivity represent areas of moderate or heavy precipitation, while areas of low dBZ indicate light precipitation, or sometimes even precipitation that is evaporating before it reaches the ground, which is known as virga (Photo 8).

In addition to determining the location and intensity of precipitation, Doppler radars across the United States use a principle known as the Doppler shift to determine whether the detected particles are moving toward or away from the radar. The Doppler shift, when applied to sound waves, is what causes the frequency (or pitch) of a siren or train whistle to change as an ambulance or locomotive moves toward or away from you. As a train moves toward you, the apparent wave-

Photo 8: Virga falling out of mid- to high-altitude clouds. Image courtesy: Jan Null.

length of the sound approaching from the whistle is shortened, leading you to hear a pitch that is higher in frequency than the actual sound. As the train moves away, the apparent wavelength of the sound is lengthened such that the sound you hear is at a lower pitch than the actual frequency emitted. Similarly, the returned microwave pulses also experience the Doppler shift when precipitation particles are moving toward or away from the radar with the wind. Using this principle, the radar can determine how fast the wind is blowing, but only along the direction of the radar beam (not across) and where precipitation is occurring. Hence Doppler radars have the capability to detect changes in wind speed. For example, when a rotating thunderstorm is detected by the radar, a "couplet" of strong inbound winds adjacent to strong outbound winds is visible (Photo 9).

United States radars also are equipped with dual-polarimetric radar, or dual-pol, technology, an even more recent advance in Doppler radar. Dual-pol radars emit two pulses: one oriented horizontally, the other oriented vertically. Differences in the returned signal in the horizontal and vertical plane can be used for a wide variety of applications, including determination of precipitation type. For example, hail is relatively large and heavy compared to raindrops, and tends to tumble as it falls. This property gives similar horizontal and vertical returned signals. Raindrops tend to fall in a more asymmetric shape, causing different reflectivity values in the horizontal and vertical directions. Therefore, it is possible to identify when hail is present in a thunderstorm as opposed to simply very large raindrops. Additionally, dual-pol radar can determine whether there is a large degree of similarity in the precipitation particles it detects. This allows for a determination of when, for example, all snow is occurring in a cloud or when rain droplets may be mixing in with snow crystals. The ability to better ascertain precipitation type and identify that all-important rain/snow line during winter storms has increased the accuracy of weather forecasts (34).

Even with all of the advances in radar technology, there are still some limitations to the equipment. For example, "overshooting" precipitation can be a problem when the reflecting targets are located at the outer reach of the radar beam. As the distance from the radar increases, so does the elevation of the radar beam. Any precipitation underneath the radar beam will not be sensed by the radar. Additionally, virga will be sensed no differently by the radar up at the level of the radar beam than percipitation which is reaching the ground. Finally, radar beams can experience blockage and interference by mountains and wind farms. Despite its limitations, radar is an invaluable tool which has greatly advanced the study and analysis of the atmosphere.

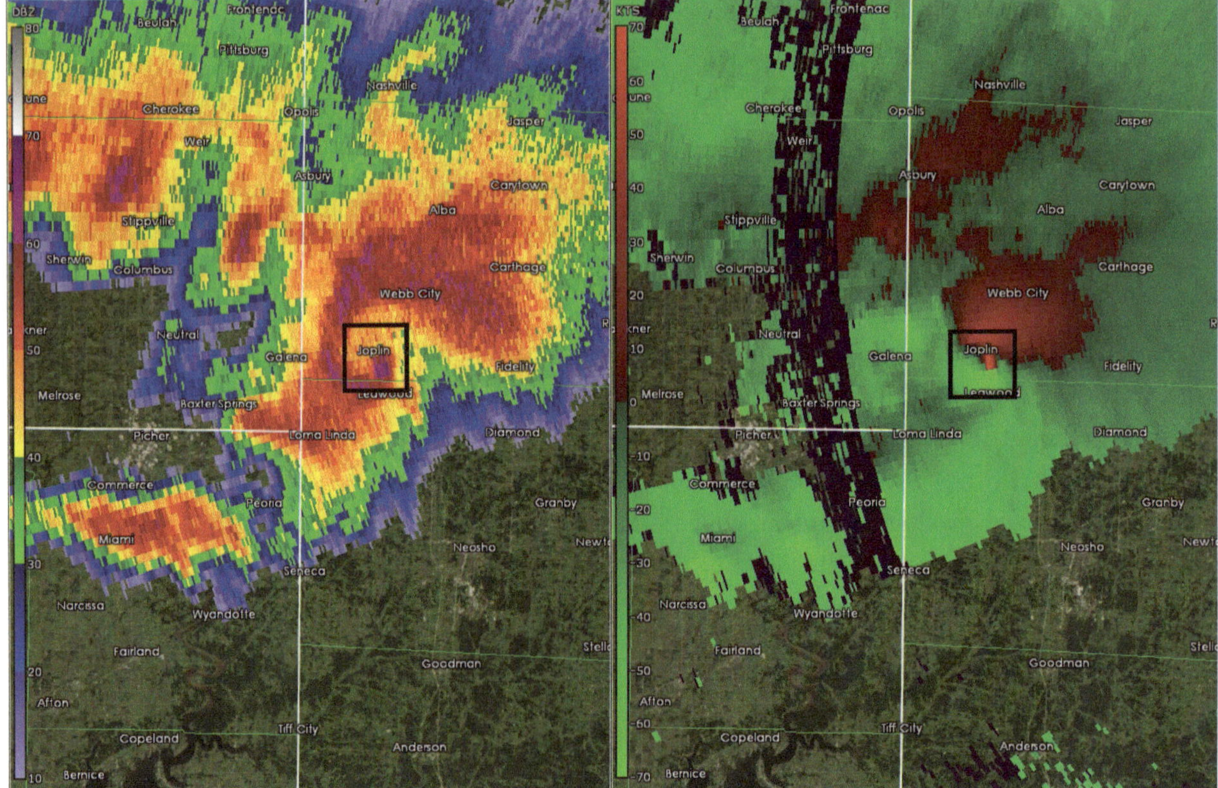

Photo 9: Doppler radar reflectivity (left) and velocity (right) imagery from the Joplin, Missouri tornado of May 22, 2011. The hook echo is visible on the reflectivity image, while strong rotation is shown in the velocity image by the bright red and green pixels over Joplin. Black box indicates area of interest.

Non-meteorological Phenomena on Radar

A Doppler radar unit sends out pulses of microwave energy as it rotates around in a circle. After each scan, it tilts upward slightly and completes another full circle. Within about six minutes, the radar creates a nearly complete three-dimensional picture of precipitation in the atmosphere. The microwave signals that are sent out bounce off of reflecting targets and back to the radar. Because the radar beam, or pulses, are sent out slightly above the horizontal, the radar senses precipitation higher and higher up in the atmosphere as one moves farther and farther away from the radar.

One common non-meteorological phenomenon is ground clutter. Tall objects that are fixed to the ground, such as mountains and tall buildings, can sometimes intercept or block the radar beam as the signal moves away from the radar. Just like precipitation particles, the radar signal can bounce off of these fixed objects and return a signal to the radar. The signal can appear as precipitation, but unlike rainfall, it remains stationary and doesn't move over time.

Seasonal "clutter mapping" is performed to correct for some of the known ground clutter and remove this problem, but it is always an issue with radar in mountainous terrain. When the radar beam intercepts sea spray associated with waves on bodies of water, it can return a non-precipitation signal as well. Just like ground clutter, this is usually only a problem with the lowest-level elevation scans that are closest to the ground surfaces. However, sea clutter tends to be much harder to map or correct for than fixed ground-clutter objects.

Another example of stationary radar echoes are those caused by wind farms. The blades of wind turbines can cover a diameter of approximately 300 feet and are mounted on towers approximately 260 feet above the ground; groups of these turbines make up a wind farm. As the blades spin and reach the topmost point of their movement, they are high enough to be picked up by the lowest-elevation radar beam. These false returns, like sea clutter, are very difficult to remove from a radar map because the rotation of the blades causes the radar to sense that these particles are moving, rather than stationary like a mountain or a building.

At various times, it is even possible to see bird migrations in real time on radar! Blue concentric circles that appear at multiple radar sites at the same time represent not precipitation, but large groups of migrating birds. At sunset, bats leaving their caves for the night can also be captured by radar. At other times, bug movements (when large quantities of, say, grasshoppers, are present) can be captured by radar!

Lightning

Lightning in the United States is detected by two ground-based systems. The National Lightning Detection Network (NLDN) is operated by Vaisala, while Earth Networks offers its own proprietary Total Lightning Network (35). By detecting radio signals from lightning strikes, ground-based sensors can determine how far away a lightning strike occurred. Triangulation, or using data from at least three sensors, allows for a precise determination of where on the ground the lightning strike occurred. These ground-based systems primarily detect cloud-to-ground lightning (36) (37).

The Geostationary Lightning Mapper (GLM) onboard the current generation of GOES satellites is capable of mapping total lightning activity, including in-cloud and cloud-to-ground (Photo 10). The camera sensor can record around 500 images per second, allowing for detailed animations of lightning in thunderstorms. Applications of GLM technology are currently being developed by research scientists.

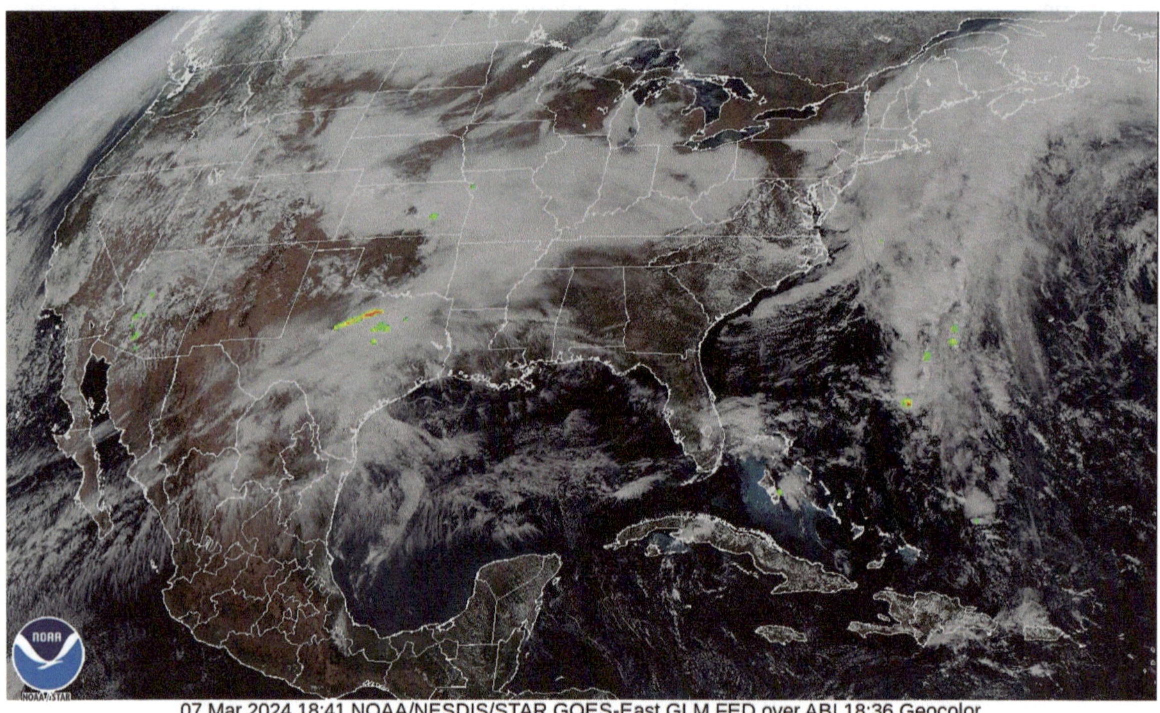

Photo 10: Visible satellite imagery overlaid with Global Lightning Mapper (GLM) data from March 7, 2024.

Volunteer Weather Observing Networks

As important as the automated and high-tech equipment are to meteorologists, there is an invaluable data source we have not yet discussed: volunteer weather observers. Even with all of the ground-based and remote sensing observations we have, it is still so important to have even more of what we call ground truth: real-time observations from actual humans on the ground. Even if every trained meteorologist took observations (and many do!), there would still be many gaps. For this reason, meteorologists, emergency managers, farmers, and more rely on networks of trained weather observers. We will discuss four of them here.

The National Weather Service Cooperative Observer program was created under the Organic Act of 1890 and is comprised of between 5,000 and 6,000 volunteer observers. These observers typically provide daily maximum and minimum temperatures, as well as 24-hour precipitation, snowfall, and snow depth reports once per day. These data support the NWS in its mission to protect lives and property, and are used in forecasting as well as in research of past weather events. In order to be certified as a Cooperative Observer site, the equipment must meet all of the NWS standards for meteorological observations, including the type of equipment used and where that equipment is located on a property (38).

Another network of volunteer weather observers is heavily relied on by meteorologists: the Community Collaborative Rain, Hail, and Snow (CoCoRaHS—pronounced Co-Co-Raaahs) network (39). It began in 1998 at the Colorado Climate Center at Colorado State University. One by one, U.S. states and territories, as well as Canada and the Bahamas, joined the network as it has grown steadily over the years. Volunteers of all ages and education levels are welcome to be a part of this network, whose mission includes providing "accurate, high-quality precipitation data to end users," while increasing citizens' weather awareness and providing resources for educators and the community at large.

Volunteers are told where to purchase a standard rain gauge needed to make observations, and then trained on how to take precipitation measurements and submit them to CoCoRaHS. Studies comparing NWS manual rain gauges to CoCoRaHS measurements have shown that there is nearly 100% accuracy—meaning that the volunteer observers are as accurate as meteorologists! Due to the limitations of automated equipment, manual observations are superior to automated ones, and thus CoCoRaHS remains a network of actual human volunteer weather observers.

CoCoRaHS continues to add observers steadily, and now has over 26,000 active volunteer observers. Observations are available in near-real time via the CoCoRaHS website, and the data is also archived at the National Centers for Environmental Information (NCEI). As a forensic meteorologist, I cannot understate the value of having these weather observations to do my job. Often, volunteers will note comments about impactful weather that has occurred since their last observation. These eyes on the ground help us construct an accurate chronology of weather events for dates in months and years past.

Types of Rain Gauges

A rain gauge, at its simplest, is a vessel to collect rain and measure how much has fallen. In theory, one could do this with any vessel: a cup, a pan, a wagon, and so forth. However, using a traditional ruler marked with inch and centimeter increments in such a vessel quickly becomes a challenge. If less than a quarter of an inch of rain falls, it is difficult, if not impossible, to read and discriminate between the marked increments.

Most volunteer observing networks use a U.S. standard rain gauge. This device consists of two nested cylinders. The rain falls into the outer cylinder and is funneled into the narrow, interior cylinder with a specially designed lid. This "stretches" the vertical scale of the rain; for example, one inch of rainfall may stretch into approximately 15 inches of vertical height. Hash marks printed on the interior cylinder allow rainfall increments as small as 0.01 of an inch to be easily read.

Another type of rain gauge that is commonly used at automated weather observing stations is called a tipping bucket rain gauge. In this type of gauge, rain is collected and dropped via a funnel onto a device that looks and works very much like a seesaw. The device is designed to tip back and forth at a certain amount of rainfall—for example, 0.01 of an inch. An automated device counts the number of times the seesaw tips back and forth to determine the total rainfall. These devices are limited because the mechanical seesaw is subject to freezing during winter, and a heater is often required to ensure year-round functionality. Additionally, if the seesaw only partially fills during one rainfall episode and then is not emptied prior to the next one, rainfall totals may be affected. If rainfall is very intense, the funnel mechanism can overflow and affect rainfall totals as well.

The weighing rain gauge is another type of automated gauge. Rather than depending on a seesaw mechanism, the gauge simply collects precipitation inside a vessel and uses a precise measurement of the weight to calculate precipitation amount. The rim of these devices is often equipped with a heater, so they can be used to collect all types of precipitation. Weighing rain gauges can be more expensive than tipping-bucket gauges, but they are not as affected by very intense rainfall.

The NWS also runs a network of volunteer weather observers known as SKYWARN®. This program, which has operated since the 1970s, trains volunteers to observe and report information on all types of weather hazards, though their main focus is severe weather such as high-wind damage, hail, and tornadoes. SKYWARN® observers attend classes twice per year in which NWS meteorologists review seasonal hazards, as well as how to identify and report damage. The program is open to the public, and many volunteers enjoy learning about local weather from NWS meteorologists (who, like most of us, are eager to talk about interesting weather to anyone who will listen).

Weather observations are also crowd sourced via the mPing network. mPing, short for Meteorological Phenomena Identification Near the Ground, is a free app that can be downloaded on most smartphones. Anyone can use the app to submit weather information anonymously. Observers report precipitation type: rain, drizzle, freezing rain, snow, and so forth (we will discuss these and other types of precipitation in Chapter 4). These reports help verify radar- and ASOS-identified precipitation type, and are particularly helpful during winter storms to determine where the rain/snow line is located. Users can also submit reports of tornadoes, hail, wind damage, visibility obstructions, and even mudslides or landslides. Although the app uses cell phone location information to pinpoint where the reports are coming from, the data remains otherwise anonymous. The app allows users to animate submitted reports on a map in real-time. The advantage of a free app like mPing is that it allows many people to quickly and easily submit reports. The disadvantage is that the reports are not submitted (generally) by trained spotters, and thus are not verified or quality controlled individually. They are most useful when viewed in an aggregate sense; if many people are submitting reports of snow falling, there is a high likelihood that snow is indeed falling in that area (Photo 11).

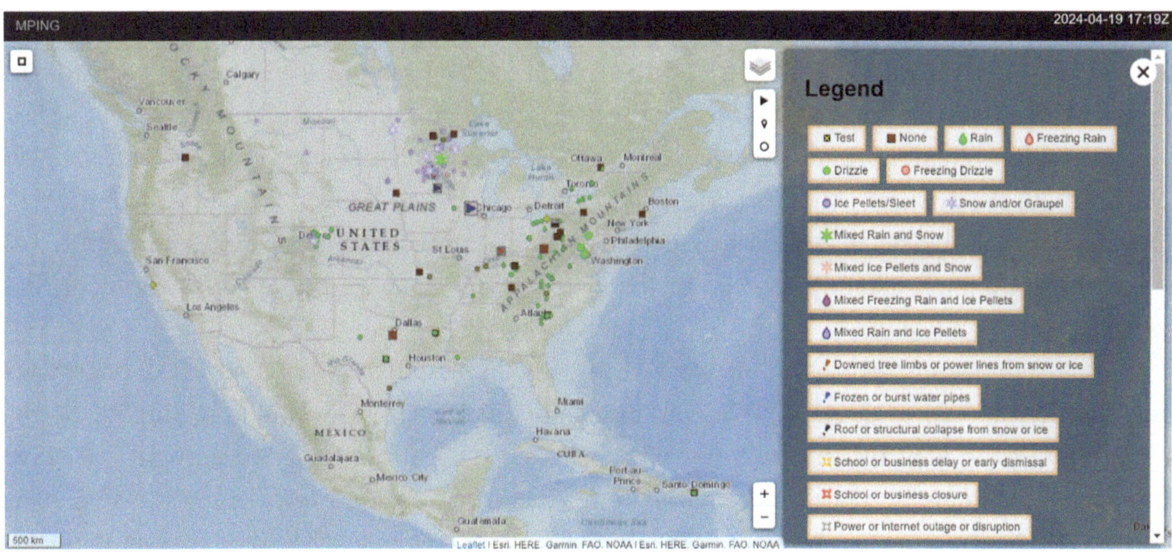

Photo 11: mPing map showing mixed precipitation types occurring on Apr 19, 2024.

Spring Topic #3: Climate Normals and Records

All this discussion of measurements and observations may have you wondering, "What is it all for?" Why would someone take measurements, day in and day out, for years or even decades? If you are a gardener, you likely already pay attention to changes in the weather over time. If a highly unusual weather event happens (heavy rain or snow, extreme cold or heat), you just know that it is something unusual. The way that you know is by having observed conditions over long periods of time. Even if you are not directly taking measurements, your brain is accumulating information to determine which conditions are typical for your area and which are highly anomalous.

As scientists, meteorologists do a similar type of analysis of weather conditions over long periods of time to understand what is typical and what may be considered extreme. In order to define whether a particular weather event is unusual or extreme, one must have a context by which to make that determination. Meteorologists use *climate normals* to define the climate of a particular region, and use that as a background against which they can evaluate individual weather events. Thirty years is the standard averaging period that meteorologists use for climate normals. In other words, when a broadcast meteorologist says, "Our normal high for this date is 72 degrees," or "Normal seasonal snowfall for this area is 60 inches," what he or she means is that the average high temperature over a 30-year time period is 72 degrees, and an average of seasonal snowfall over 30 winters is 60 inches.

Why 30 years, and not 50, or 100, or 1,000? The 30-year averaging period was defined by the World Meteorological Organization (WMO), the governing body for international meteorology, in the 1930s. The reason for a 30-year averaging period was that this was a length of time over which most countries had reliable climate records (40). The WMO also recommends that normals be recalculated once every decade to account for longer-term changes in Earth's climate. For example, what was typical for an area in the 1950s may not be typical for that same place in today's climate. Thus, U.S. climate normals are calculated for a 30-year time period and republished every decade (41).

The current climate normals were released in 2021 and cover the averaging period from 1991 through 2020; the averages will be recalculated again in 2030 and cover the period from 2001 to 2030. Normals can be calculated for any period of time: annual, monthly, daily, and even hourly! Temperatures can be broken down even further into average daily high temperature, average daily low temperature, and so on.

How are climate normals used? As we have already discussed, they set a context or background against which we can evaluate how uncommon individual weather events are. Climate normals are used not just to identify uncommon events, but also to identify periods of drought, excessively rainy periods, extreme heat, and more. Climate normals are also used to plan for seasonal energy usage and to determine when to plant crops. Individual citizens may even look at climate normals to decide where to take a vacation and what to pack.

Finally, climate normals are used to identify long-term changes in the climate. For example, we can look at how many daily rainfall records are set over a year to determine whether extreme rainfall events are becoming more common (42), or identify whether increased atmospheric heat due to greenhouse gasses has manifested in warmer daily maximum temperatures, warmer overnight low temperatures, or both (43). Many long-term observing stations have documented a statistically significant increase in daily minimum temperatures over time, meaning that nights are not getting as cold as they used to.

In addition to knowing what the average conditions are at a particular location, it is important to understand ranges and extremes to fully assess the climate and identify changes over time. Earlier, we discussed two cities: Seattle and Bismarck. These two cities experience very different ranges of temperature over a year despite being at similar latitudes, with Bismarck having the larger seasonal variation due to its location in the middle of a land mass. Now let's take a look at the temperature records, or all-time highest and lowest recorded temperatures, for both cities. Seattle's hottest official temperature is an impressive 108 degrees Fahrenheit which occurred on June 28, 2021, while the all-time coldest temperature is zero degrees Fahrenheit which occurred on January 31, 1950 (44). In Bismarck, the all-time record high temperature is 114 degrees Fahrenheit (July 6, 1936) and the all-time record low is -45 degrees Fahrenheit, which occurred on both January 13, 1916, and February 16, 1936 (21). While Bismarck and Seattle have similar all-time record highs, it can get much colder in Bismarck than Seattle. If you happened to be "lucky" enough to be in each city when their all-time record low temperatures are broken, you would need to wear many more layers in Bismarck!

Weather can be a lot like baseball: if you have a question, there is probably a statistic to answer it. What are the odds of a white Christmas anywhere in the United States? The NWS keeps track of that (45). What is the longest stretch of days without rain in Portland, Oregon? It is 71 days (46). The great thing about long-term temperature, precipitation, and snowfall observations is that many weather and climate questions can be answered with a little (or sometimes a lot) of mathematical analysis of the extensive database.

Spring Topic #4: Scales of Motion and Wind Systems

As we start to look in detail at the local weather, one of the things we notice is that there are weather features on many different size scales. A broadcast meteorologist may show a satellite animation on which we can see visible swirls the size of continents. Similarly, if we walk around a building on a windy fall day, we can also see swirls and eddies as the leaves are blown around the building, on a much smaller scale than on the satellite animation.

There are four scales of motions in the atmosphere: microscale, mesoscale, synoptic scale, and global or planetary scale (Figure 15). Microscale motions are the smallest and are comprised of tiny swirls and circulations that result from friction as air flows past trees, mountains, buildings, and other barriers. The lifespan of atmospheric circulations tends to be related to their scale. Microscale circulations have the shortest lifespan, of only seconds to minutes. The next-largest atmospheric motions are mesoscale circulations, which are on the order of tens of miles across and last anywhere from several minutes to several hours. Examples of mesoscale circulations include tornadoes, waterspouts, and even longer-lived dust devils. Individual thunderstorms are generally considered to be mesoscale features, as are the thermally driven circulations we discussed in Chapter 1, sea breezes and mountain/valley breezes.

Next largest in size are synoptic scale circulations, which tend to last several days and can be hundreds to up to a thousand miles across. All but the smallest hurricanes are generally considered to be on the small end of the synoptic scale motions, and individual high- and low-pressure systems in the midlatitudes that impact much of the continental United States are also synoptic scale features. Planetary scale features are the largest and longest-lived of all, and include waves in the jet stream, which can persist for weeks and create long-lived weather impacts such as drought, heat waves, and persistent rainfall over weeks to months.

As we previously discussed, there are many forces that push and pull molecules in the atmosphere to determine which way the wind blows. As the scale of atmospheric motion changes, which forces are most important and largest in magnitude change as well. Small scale circulations, such

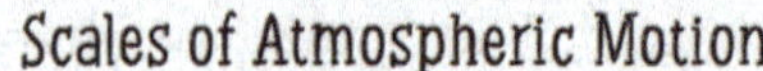

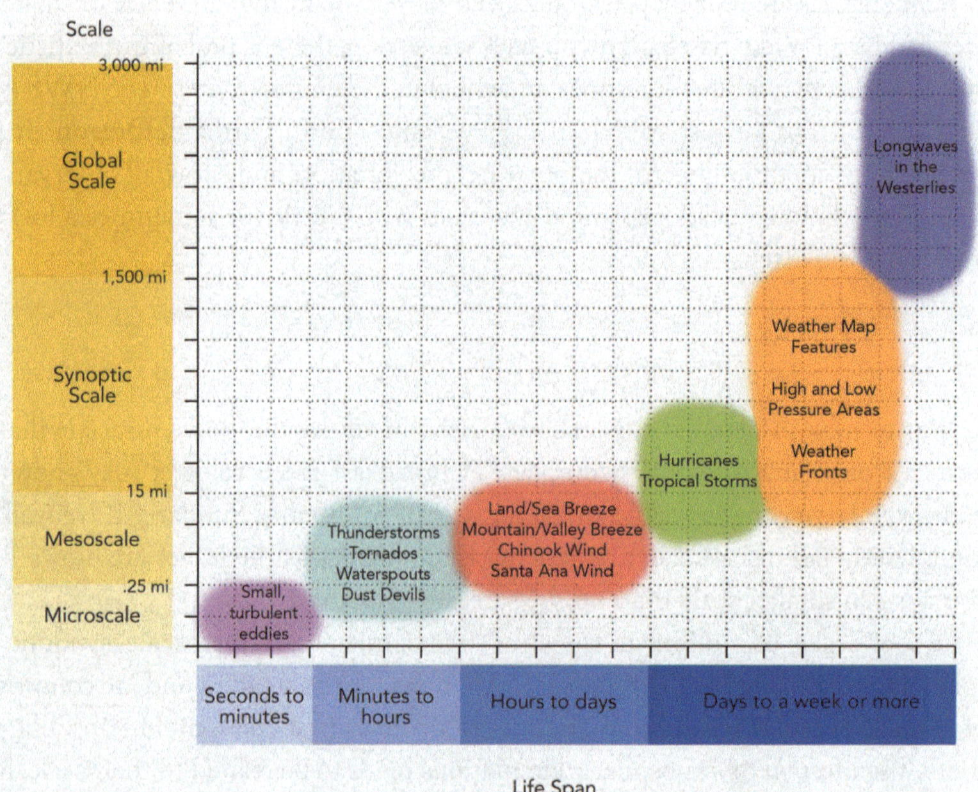

Figure 15

as tornadoes and dust devils, are governed by *cyclostrophic balance*. Here, the two most important forces are the pressure gradient force and centrifugal force; the latter is the outward-pushing force that anyone who has taken a turn on an exit ramp just a little too fast has doubtless experienced. Even though tornadoes happen on a rotating earth, their time scale is so short that the Coriolis force (discussed in Chapter 1) is not important in governing the winds in those circulations.

Synoptic scale features above the surface, where friction is negligible, are governed by *geostrophic balance* (where airflow is in a straight line) or *gradient balance* (for curved motion). In this case, the two most prominent forces governing where the wind blows are Coriolis force and pressure gradient force. For curved airflow, centrifugal force is also important. Synoptic scale features last long enough that they are affected by the Earth's rotation, and thus the Coriolis effect must be included when calculating motions on the synoptic scale and larger.

Why is this important? If one is interested in a weather forecast, it is necessary to know the appropriate equation of atmospheric motion for the scale of the features you are looking to forecast, and then accurately solve those equations stepping forward in time. Motions become more chaotic as the scale of motion decreases, so it is currently impossible to predict where features such as dust devils will form and how they will move. By contrast, computers and better-quality, more frequent observations over the past 30 years have allowed for considerable increases in forecast skill for synoptic scale features. A dramatic example of this improvement is seen in tropical cyclone (including hurricane) forecasts. With the data input to the numerical models from satellites, radar, aircraft observations, surface observations, dropsondes, and even drones, there has been a huge improvement of tropical cyclone track forecasts since the 1970s, from 24-hour forecasts through five-day forecasts (47). Forecasts of the intensity of hurricanes and tropical cyclones have improved over time as well, but have not seen as great of an improvement as hurricane track forecasts. Partly this is because the factors that are responsible for the intensification and weakening of tropical storms are still not captured fully by the current forecast models, while the airflow patterns that determine a particular cyclone track are generally much better simulated.

Wrap-up: Spring

In this chapter, we learned about the many scales and structures of atmospheric motion, scratched the surface (garden pun intended) on the many data sources that are used to observe the atmosphere, and learned how the data is used to understand long-term climate conditions. Spring is the season where things are just ramping up in the garden, and the same is true in this book! In the next chapters, we will take a deep dive into some of the most common topics we are asked about as meteorologists.

Gardener Goals

- Commit to tracking plant progress on your property for one full growing season. Pick five types of plants to track: it could be perennials which have been cut back to the ground for the winter, large deciduous trees such as maples or oaks, shrubs, or even annuals or vegetables which you plant on a certain date from transplants or seed. Track parameters such as when leaves first appear, when buds and flowers appear, how long flowers last, any pest problems that arise, and when the plants die off or go dormant at the end of the growing season.
- Start tracking one weather parameter on your property. I recommend temperature or precipitation. See the appendix in this book for guidelines and best practices for taking weather observations in your backyard.
- Look up the monthly climate normals (temperature and precipitation) for the closest weather station to where you live (ncei.noaa.gov/access/us-climate-normals/). Compare the changing day-to-day weather conditions against the normals and records.

Chapter 3

Summer

Summer Gardening: Increasing Dependence on the Weather

Ahhh, summer. As I sit at my writing desk, we have been enjoying a seemingly endless stretch of sunny days, perfect temperatures, and low humidity. Of course, we've had occasional rainfall and hot/humid days, but overall, the past couple of months have been characterized by almost too-perfect summer weather.

While this has been excellent for outdoor events, gardens and lawns all across the Northeast are suffering from a lack of rain. Drought can be insidious, and unless you are dependent on regular rainfall for a livelihood (agriculture, for example) or you're an aficionado of a lush, green lawn, it may be something that goes unnoticed.

On the other side of the coin, I can recall summers with exactly the opposite problem: too much rainfall. Of all the seasons, summer seems to be the one when my garden is most at the mercy of the weather. I don't know if I have ever lived through a year where I have said to myself, "Well, now, that has been the perfect amount of rainfall, delivered at perfect intervals!"

Regardless of what the weather does, there are always issues a gardener must confront. As Danish philosopher Kierkegaard said, "Life is not a problem to solve, but a reality to be experienced." What is true in life is also true in gardening: thinking of the weather conditions and other issues as problems to be dealt with make the whole process of growing a garden confrontational and discouraging. Rather, looking at weather events (and other situations) as experiences to be worked through frames the process in a much more positive light. In fact, I would even go so far as to say that the need to go through experiences, enjoy successes, and work through problems is one of the reasons I enjoy gardening so much. All of the frustrations and hard work pay off when I am able to enjoy the fruits, and vegetables, of my labor (Photo 12)!

Photo 12: Home-grown produce. Top row: not-yet-ripe figs on my potted fig tree, a nearly-ready fig, and that delightful bite of the first ripe fig of the season. Second row: seeds saved from my Nonni's garden, newly planted seeds in peat pellets, just waiting to emerge, and newly transplanted tomatoes and beans in my outside garden. Middle row: spaghetti squash, which takes nearly all season to fully ripen, overcrowded-but-very-healthy red lettuce and snap peas, and my Nonni's green beans, which grew longer than my arm. Fourth row: healthy herb pots on my patio which produce all season long, one batch of basil ready to turn into pesto, and newly harvested lettuce, rosemary, parsley, and basil. Bottom row: rainbow carrots which tasted delicious and produced abundantly, various types of tomatoes, and my one and only batch of peppers which grew large enough to enjoy.

Summer Topic #1: Humidity and Condensation

A common question we are asked as meteorologists is to explain the enormous variety of cloud forms that we see in the sky (Photo 13). It is amazing to think that simple water droplets and ice crystals suspended in the atmosphere can create everything from wispy cirrus clouds to enormous black thunderstorm clouds. The short answer to the question "Why am I seeing the types of clouds I see in the sky today?" is, simply, atmospheric stability. I say *short* a bit tongue-in-cheek, because in reality students spend a great deal of time during undergraduate meteorology programs trying to understand the topic of atmospheric stability. I was one of those students, and I can vouch for the fact that this is one of the topics that can be simple on its surface but very difficult to understand when we begin to dig into the math and physics!

Stability is simplest to understand when one considers the example of *gravitational stability*. Imagine a ball sitting in a valley as shown in Figure 16. If you were to give the ball a gentle tap, which way would it initially go? Up the hill, of course! However, without your hand to push it again, where would the ball want to go? Back down the hill! This illustrates a stable situation. In a stable environment, the tendency of the ball, in the absence of your hand forcing it up the hill, is to roll back from where it came.

A stable atmosphere is analogous to the ball in a stable gravitational environment. In the absence of a push, or forcing mechanism, the *tendency* of the air is to go back from where it came. When the atmosphere is stable, air that is forced upward is colder than the surrounding environment. Cold air is denser than warm air, and thus air that is colder than its surroundings will have a tendency to sink downward, unless it is forced to rise. This is analogous to your hand continually forcing the ball uphill, when it would go back downhill if you remove your hand. Air can be forced to rise upward over mountainous terrain, or frontal zones where warm air is being pushed up on top of cold air (we will cover fronts in more detail in Chapter 4). When the atmosphere is stable, clouds tend to take on a horizontally layered appearance, and are known as stratiform clouds.

Let us return to our ball example again to envision the opposite. Now let us imagine that the ball is sitting exactly on the crest of a hill (Figure 16). We give the ball a gentle tap again. Where will the ball go? In this case, it would accelerate, or speed up, down the hill, away from its original position. Not only is the ball moving away, or in the direction of the initial push, but it is accelerating as well.

Air parcels, or bubbles of air in the atmosphere, can be thought of in a similar manner. If an air parcel is warmer than its environment, it is buoyant and will want to rise upward. Helium balloons rise upward on the same principle: helium is lighter than most other atmospheric gasses, and thus a helium balloon is buoyant and will rise if a child is not careful and lets go. I had such a bad track record with balloons that my mother took to tying them to my wrist or coat to avoid the inevitable tears that resulted from my inability to hang on to them!

This situation, illustrated by the ball on the hill and rising balloon examples, is what we consider unstable. In an unstable environment, air will accelerate upward because it is warmer than its

Photo 13: Top: Standing lenticular cloud at sunset, looking north from Joshua Tree. Bottom: Spectacular Kelvin-Helmholtz wave clouds over Mt. Montara, California. Images courtesy: Jan Null.

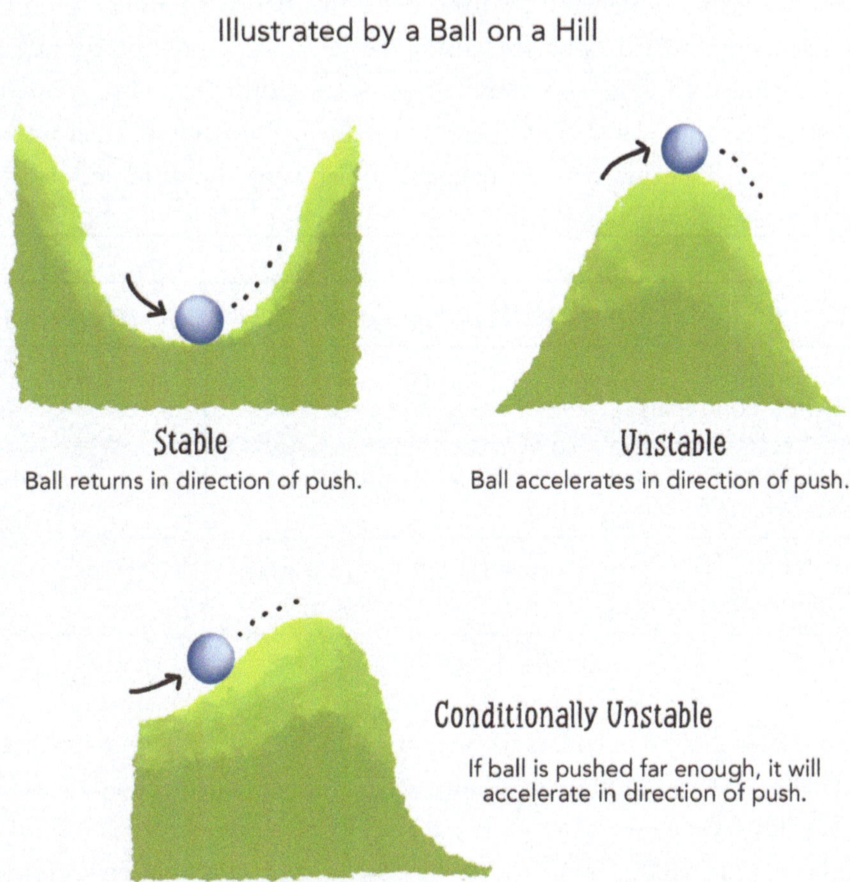

Figure 16

surroundings. Unstable environments lead to the development of cumuliform clouds, whose visual appearance is starkly different from stratiform clouds. Cumuliform clouds have a puffy, almost cauliflower-like appearance.

To be precise, the unstable situation we describe above is *absolute instability*. In the real atmosphere, we typically observe a hybrid situation, or *conditional instability*. Let's imagine a ball sitting on a flat surface with a hill in its path (Figure 16). If you give the ball a gentle tap, not enough of a push to reach the crest of the hill, the ball will find itself in a stable situation and sink backward to where it came from. However, if there is enough of a push for the ball to reach the top of the hill, it will find itself in an unstable situation and accelerate away from the direction of the push.

In the atmosphere, air generally has to be forced to a certain altitude, known as the level of free convection, in order to become unstable. If there isn't enough upward forcing, or push, on a given day, then there may be stratiform clouds or even no clouds. However, if the air can be forced high enough up in the atmosphere, it will accelerate upward and form cumuliform clouds and even thunderstorms. Meteorologists use the level of free convection and numerous other parameters to evaluate the atmospheric stability on a particular day and determine the likelihood of thunderstorm formation.

All of this discussion on atmospheric stability has laid the foundation for talking about the fun stuff: cloud classification! Clouds are generally classified according to two parameters: altitude and environmental stability. Thus, most cloud charts that one can download freely off the internet take the form of some kind of a grid, with lovely visuals illustrating the different cloud types (48). They can all be simply broken down as follows:

Altitude	*Cumuliform Cloud Types*	*Stratiform Cloud Types*
High clouds (cloud base over 20,000 feet)	Cirrocumulus	Cirrus, cirrostratus
Midlevel clouds (cloud base 6,500-20,000 feet)	Altocumulus	Altostratus
Low clouds (cloud base under 6,500 feet)	Cumulus, cumulonimbus*	Stratus, nimbostratus

Table 1: Basic cloud types.

As with most attempts by scientists to categorize and classify phenomena, there are numerous exceptions and hybrids. For example, cumulonimbus, or thunderstorm, clouds (noted with an asterisk in the table) generally have a low cloud base, but the clouds themselves can extend to the top of the troposphere, upwards of 30,000 feet because they form in an unstable environment where the air accelerates upward. Stratocumulus clouds are not shown in the table above since they are a sort of hybrid classification of layered clouds which can form in areas of complex atmospheric stability (49).

Clouds can be tagged with descriptors to further classify them. For example, any cloud with a *nimbo* or *nimbus* in the name has precipitation falling out of it. Altocumulus *castellanus* clouds have vertical, tower-like growths protruding from their tops. Cumulus *congestus*, or towering cumulus clouds, are more vertically developed than fair-weather cumulus clouds, and may eventually grow into cumulonimbus clouds.

Then there are cloud types that defy classification in a nice grid. Lenticular clouds are mountain-wave clouds that form when air is forced up and over high mountains (Photo 13). Pyrocumulus clouds form as a result of the extreme heat from wildfires. Aircraft condensation trails are even a type of cloud that form due to jet exhaust.

In years past, human weather observers took observations and were trained to estimate cloud height, identify cloud type, and determine what fraction of the sky was cloud covered. Today, automated ASOS sensors have equipment to identify cloud levels and cloud cover, although when cloud type is important, the automated observations can be supplemented with human remarks—for example, FC is used to identify a funnel cloud, a feature the sensors cannot identify but which indicates visible rotation is occurring in a thunderstorm. An automated sensor known as a ceilometer is used at ASOS sites to measure cloud height. The sensor identifies obstructions to vertical visibility (such as clouds) and then algorithms are used to calculate the height of those obscurations. Both automated and manually observed cloud covers are categorized into *oktas*, or eighths, and described as shown in Table 2.

Oktas (eighths of sky obscured by clouds)	*Cloud Cover*
0	Clear
Up to 2/8 (or 1/4) obscured	Few clouds
Above 2/8 (or 1/4) to 4/8 (1/2) obscured	Scattered clouds
Above 4/8 (1/2) up to but not including 8/8 (full) obscuration	Broken clouds
8/8 Full obscuration	Overcast

Table 2: Cloud cover definitions.

ASOS sensors are capable of identifying multiple levels of obscurations, which is useful for when there are various cloud types and levels of cloud cover at different altitudes. If you keep a weather or gardening journal, try to note the cloud types and the amount of cloud cover you observe on a regular basis. Eventually, you will learn how cloud type and amount relates to the weather you observe in your area as well!

Summer Topic #2: Fog

Of all of the weather topics which we discuss in this book, it may seem odd that fog merits an entire section all of its own. After all, fog isn't really what we would consider high-impact weather in a garden. However, fog is a very high-impact weather hazard when it occurs on roadways, particularly interstate highways. Sudden changes in visibility can result in multi-car pileups and countless injuries and fatalities. Fog can also wreak havoc on flight schedules and even trains.

Fog is often described as a cloud whose base is at or near the ground, and that definition is technically correct. The National Weather Service defines fog as "water droplets suspended in air at the Earth's surface" (50). In order to be defined as fog, the droplets must result in visibility of less than ⅝ mile. If the visibility is ⅝ of a mile or up to seven statute miles (visibility is given in eighth of a mile increments) then it is reported as mist.

All that is required to create fog is to bring the air near or at ground level to its saturation point. There are two ways in which this process can happen: water vapor can be added to the air, or the air can be cooled. Both of these processes will bring the air closer to its saturation point and increase the relative humidity; once 100 percent relative humidity is reached, condensation will occur and fog will form.

In the real atmosphere, there are a multitude of ways to bring air at the ground to saturation. When warm, moist air blows over a colder surface, the air right at ground level is cooled to its dew point. This is *advection fog*, and it occurs frequently in the San Francisco Bay as warm air moves across the cold ocean.

Another process in which the air is cooled to its dew point is during the formation of *radiation fog*. This type of fog can occur anywhere as nighttime cooling causes the air temperature to drop to the dew point. One example of radiation fog occurring is after a day when summer thunderstorms or a heavy rainfall leave behind a very moist air mass at the surface. The air is already very close to the dew point, and just a slight drop in temperature after sunset can be enough to create radiation fog. Where I live in the Hudson River valley of New York State, we often see radiation fog on fall mornings in the river valleys. Cold air sinks down from the high terrain overnight into the valleys, and fog forms when the air cools to the dew point. It makes for stunning morning views from my vantage point on the east slopes of the valley. Once the sun comes up and heats the air, the fog eventually dissipates—just after the morning rush hour, of course!

Another way air can be cooled is by forcing it to rise upward. This can occur when air is forced up the side of a mountain slope, forming *upslope fog*. Depending on the reference point, you could be looking down at it from the mountaintop, or upward at it from the lower elevations.

Another type of fog forms as a result of adding water vapor to the air (versus cooling its temperature); this is known as *steam fog*. You may have even seen this phenomenon if you were looking out at an unfrozen pond or lake on a cold fall or winter morning. Cold air becomes saturated very readily as it sits over a warmer body of water. Another situation when steam fog can be seen is when frigid Arctic air moves out over the relatively warm Atlantic waters along the East Coast of the United States.

Summer Topic #3: Weather Patterns and General Circulation of the Atmosphere

Why do some storms become large and fierce, while others are not? Why do we have long periods of dry weather that create drought? Why are there deserts in some parts of the world and rainforests in others? The answer to these questions and more lies in what meteorologists call the general circulation of the atmosphere.

As we have discussed, the reason we have atmospheric circulations at all is because the sun heats the Earth's surface unevenly; more direct heating occurs in the tropics, and less direct heating occurs at the poles. The atmosphere and oceans are forever trying to equalize this heating imbalance by moving warmer air and water toward the poles, and colder air and water from the poles to the tropics. Although individual weather systems are transient, there are preferred patterns that appear when one examines the long-term average winds and temperatures around the globe. In areas where airflow at low levels is often converging, or coming together, there tends to be rising motion. Rising air expands and cools, eventually creating clouds and precipitation, while sinking air compresses and warms. Where air diverges, or spreads out, at low levels, sinking vertical motion prevails and overall conditions tend to be dry.

Global Circulations

Figure 17 shows the idealized wind and pressure patterns over the globe. At the poles, high pressure tends to dominate, while the opposite is true near the equator. As one would expect, the tropics receive much more precipitation annually than the poles do. The common, or colloquial, name for the wet, humid area near the equator is the doldrums. Meteorologists refer to this location as the Intertropical Convergence Zone, or ITCZ, due to the fact that air comes together near the surface from both hemispheres here. Many of the world's rainforests are located in the tropics, between about 30 degrees north latitude and 30 degrees south latitude. As thunderstorms form when air converges near the surface and rises upward through the troposphere, it eventually reaches the tropopause about ten miles above the surface and spreads outward, moving toward the poles in both hemispheres. The Coriolis force deflects these upper-level winds such that a westerly jet stream develops at about 30 degrees latitude (more on jet streams shortly).

In addition to dominant high-pressure areas at both poles, there also tends to be high pressure and a sinking motion in both hemispheres at about 30 degrees latitude. Known as the subtropical highs, this region is where most of the world's deserts are located. Fair, sunny conditions and light winds are the most common weather in these areas, known as the horse latitudes. Between the subtropical high pressure and the equatorial low pressure, surface winds tend to blow toward the equator generally from the east; from the northeast in the northern hemisphere, and the southeast in the southern hemisphere. During the Age of Exploration in the 1400s and 1500s, sailing ships in this latitude band up to about 30 degrees north found themselves able to make excellent time from Europe to the Americas, and thus these prevailing winds became known as the trade winds.

In the band known as the midlatitudes, from about 30 to 60 degrees latitude, warm air moving out of the subtropical highs meets cold air coming out of the polar high and a boundary known as the polar front exists. There is another jet stream located above the polar front, appropriately known as the polar front jet stream, and it governs the path and intensity of many storms we experience in the midlatitudes.

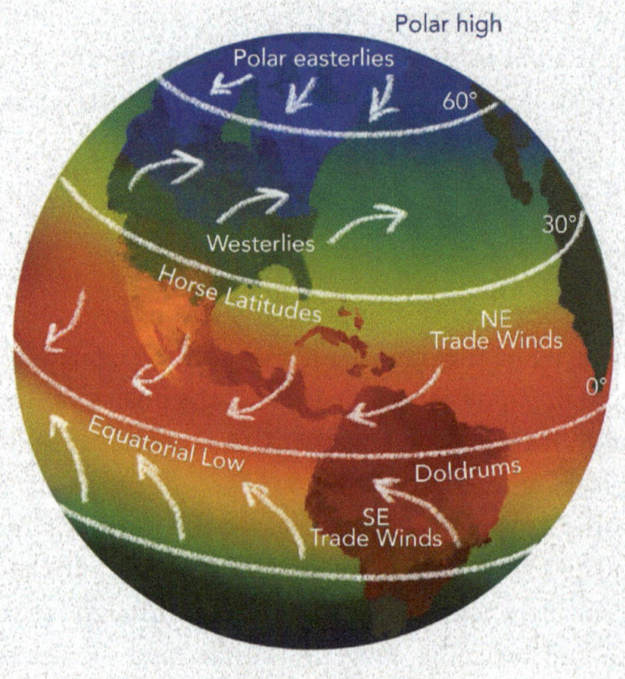

Figure 17

Jet Streams

A jet stream is defined as a rapidly moving "ribbon" of air above the surface. Jet streams can circumnavigate the entire globe, and wind speeds can vary within the jet stream. Wind speeds in the jet stream can reach, and even exceed, 150 miles per hour.

Over the United States, two primary jet streams influence the weather. The southernmost, or subtropical jet stream, tends to be located on the northern flank of the subtropical highs. With a strong subtropical jet stream, the southern United States, from Southern California all the way to the Southeast, can experience heavy rainfall. The polar front jet stream is generally located above wherever the polar front is located at the surface. In the summertime, the polar front jet stream retreats north into Canada; during the winter season, the polar front jet stream can be found as far south as Florida! When the polar front jet drops far to the south, it often brings with it cold air from the Arctic and unseasonably cold weather, even for winter. Conversely, when the polar front jet and associated surface polar front lift northward, anomalously warm conditions exist.

Just as a ribbon can be straight or weave up and down, the jet streams can also have waves or be very straight. When the jet stream is moving mostly straight from west to east, it is known as zonal flow. When the jet stream is zonal, or less amplified, surface weather systems tend to be weak and fast-moving. When the jet stream develops large waves, it can cause the development of energetic storms. Occasionally, the subtropical jet stream and the polar front jet stream can interact. When this happens, vertical circulations can become further enhanced, and some of the strongest winter storms involve interactions between the two jet streams.

Teleconnections

In the previous sections we covered a general overview of the major atmospheric circulations and jet streams. As you might imagine, there are many nuances, and the actual level of complexity of some of these features can require a graduate degree to understand! *Teleconnections*—relationships or links between weather phenomena at widely separated locations on earth—are one example of the very complex ways that the atmosphere and ocean interact. Sometimes, a strengthening or weakening of one feature can have far-reaching effects around the globe.

One example of teleconnections is the El Niño Southern Oscillation (ENSO), which is an oscillation of the surface temperatures in the tropical Pacific Ocean. The first half of the **EN**SO acronym, *El Niño,* refers to the state of ocean temperatures in the eastern tropical Pacific Ocean, along the west coast of South America. In this part of the Pacific, very strong upward movement of cold water toward the ocean surface typically keeps the ocean temperatures relatively cool. However, as early as the 1600s, fishermen noticed an episodic warming of the waters in this area, which had a direct, negative effect on the fishing industry (51). This warm period often occurred in conjunction with the Christmas holiday, hence the name El Niño, which refers to the birth of Jesus. When the waters in this area of the Pacific become warmer than normal, we call it an El Niño episode; when the waters become colder than normal it is referred to as a La Niña.

During neutral conditions, the trade winds on either side of the equator blow from east to west, thus moving warm ocean water in the same direction across the equatorial Pacific Ocean. As a result, the warm water at the ocean surface is replace by colder water from below through a process known as *upwelling.* During an El Niño episode, the trade winds weaken, decreasing the push of warm water from east to west and preventing cold water from upwelling and resulting in the warmer waters first noticed by local fishermen. During a La Niña episode, the reverse happens: trade winds strengthen, as does upwelling on the eastern side of the equatorial Pacific. As a result, ocean waters in this area become colder than usual. These ocean temperature oscillations between colder- and warmer-than-normal are directly connected to changes in the surface air pressure in the tropical Pacific Ocean. This reversal of the air pressure pattern is known as the *Southern Oscillatio*n, the latter half of the EN**SO** acronym. The combination of oscillating ocean temperatures and surface air pressures together are known as El Niño Southern Oscillation, or ENSO. If you live in the United States, it is not easy to understand why the ocean temperatures and air pressure in the tropical eastern Pacific Ocean matter for your day-to-day weather. In reality, these small oscillations in the Pacific affect weather patterns all around the world; this is why scientists spend a great deal of time monitoring the state of ENSO and forecasting the same.

In the United States, the teleconnections are strongest in the southern United States (Figure 18). During the El Niño (warm) phase of the oscillation, a stronger than normal subtropical jet stream brings wet weather to Southern California and the Gulf Coast. During a La Niña episode a strong, quasi-stationary high pressure, known as a blocking high, develops south of Alaska and allows colder air to move down from Canada into the United States.

Figure 18a

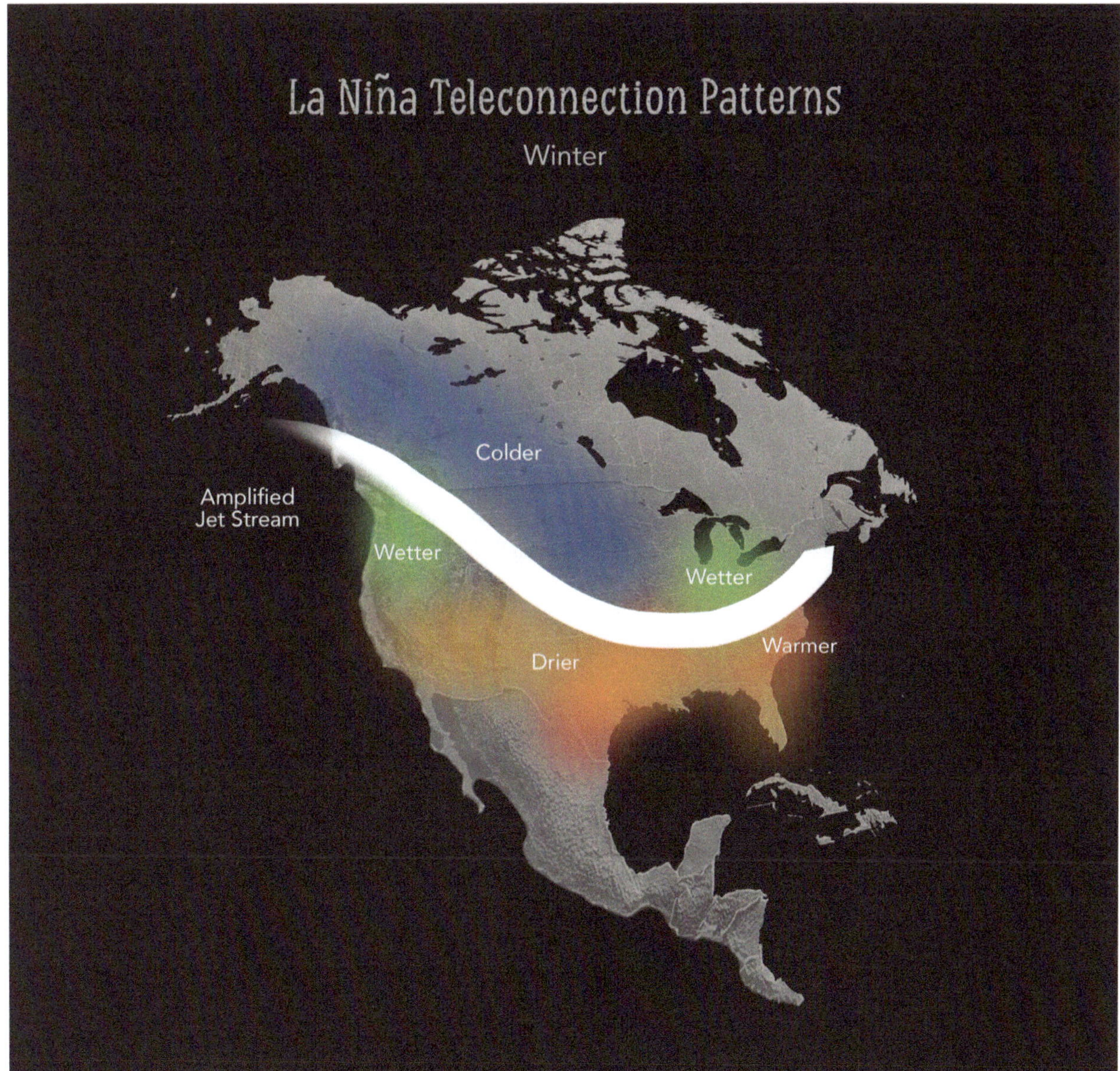

Figure 18b

Where I live in the Northeast United States, ENSO teleconnections are not as strong as in other areas of the country. However, there are other atmospheric pressure oscillations that do have strong teleconnections signals over the Northeast United States. One of these is the North Atlantic Oscillation (NAO). When the NAO is in its positive phase, a strong westerly jet stream is present in the Northern Atlantic Ocean (Figure 19). This tends to cause storms to move quickly up the East Coast and out to sea, and so here in New York we tend to see mild conditions and relatively few coastal storms, or Nor'easters. When the NAO turns to its negative phase, meteorologists along the Eastern Seaboard, especially those who love snow, start to get excited! A weaker-than-normal North Atlantic jet stream and blocking high pressure over Greenland allow the storm track to more closely follow the coast, and the storms to move more slowly, giving them time to intensify before moving offshore.

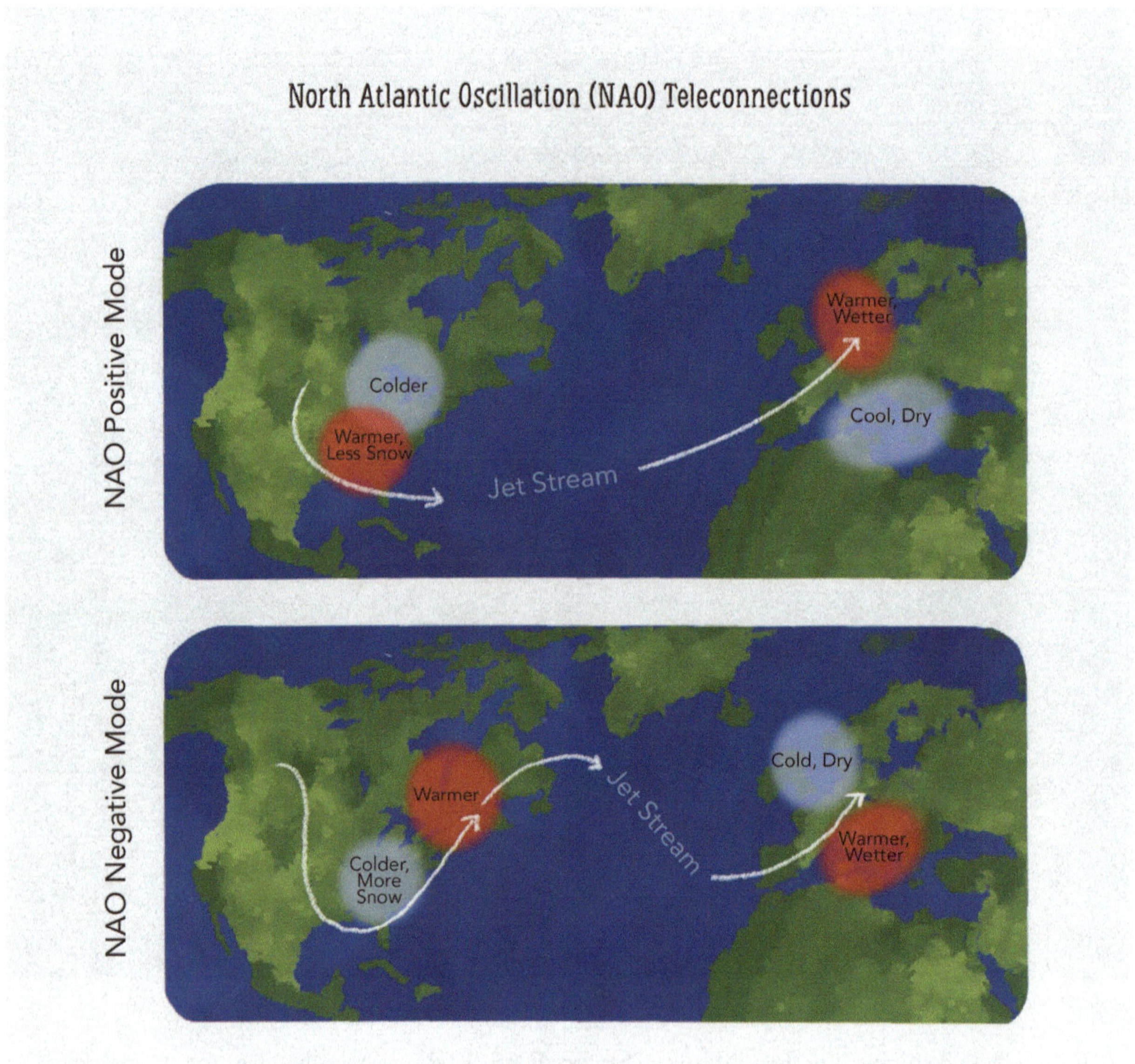

Figure 19

There are countless other oscillations in the atmosphere that meteorologists are studying to better understand teleconnections and their impacts. These include the Arctic Oscillation, Pacific Decadal Oscillation, and the Madden-Julian Oscillation. Additionally, scientists are studying long-term changes in these oscillations to better understand changes in how heat is transferred from the tropics to the poles.

Summer Topic #4: Thunderstorms and Hurricanes

Thunderstorm Basics

As a child, one of my favorite things to do during thunderstorms was sit on the front porch with my dad and watch the lightning and listen to the thunder. Although I did not know then that I would become a meteorologist, I always had a strong curiosity to learn about how thunderstorms worked. I used to have a little book about weather, entitled Weather: A Golden Guide, which I read and reread. Like most kids, I skipped past the front chapters on solar energy, radiation, and the composition of the atmosphere right to the pictures of cloud types, weather maps, and, of course, thunderstorms. I returned over and over to the illustrations that showed lightning striking a plane or how a tornado could drive straw into a tree. Fast forward twenty years, and some of my favorite classes in college were the one that covered the mechanics of thunderstorms.

Some individuals, unfortunately, have experienced or been directly impacted by severe weather and were motivated to study meteorology from there. For many of us, simply watching the sky during thunderstorms, as I did with my dad, is how we first became interested in weather. While I was in college, the original movie *Twister* (1996; a sequel, *Twisters*, was released in the summer of 2024) came out and produced a whole new generation of atmospheric science and meteorology students in the 2000s. Thunderstorms and severe weather are often the first entry point into the study of meteorology. Even among non-meteorologists, thunderstorms and tornadoes are a topic of widespread interest. When I taught a general-education meteorology course at my local community college, the unit that always created the most engagement was the one on thunderstorms.

Thunderstorms can be one of the most challenging weather phenomena for gardeners to deal with. Not only can they bring wide-ranging hazards from lightning, to strong winds, to flooding rain, but they often come up suddenly. Even if thunderstorms are in the forecast for your general area, it does not necessarily mean that a thunderstorm will impact your exact location on that day. While there are some basic steps you can take to safeguard your plants, unfortunately, protecting home gardens against severe thunderstorms can be difficult.

At its simplest, a thunderstorm is defined as any storm that produces lightning and thunder. Lightning is simply a discharge of static electricity from a storm cloud. Anyone who lives in a relatively dry climate may have had the following experience: you walk across a carpeted surface, scuffing your feet. When you touch a doorknob or other metal object, you receive an electric shock as the static electricity discharges between your finger and the door. Lightning strikes are likewise discharges of electricity, although of much larger magnitude than what occurs when your hand touches a doorknob. Lightning strikes discharge so much electricity, in fact, that the air surrounding the lightning strike is heated to over 50,000 degrees Fahrenheit! When this happens, the air rapidly expands and produces a shock wave, which moves away from the lightning strike. When this wave reaches our ear, we hear thunder.

Why do some clouds electrify and produce lightning strikes? Static electricity, in general, is a result of separation of charge between objects. All atoms contain electrons, or negatively charged particles. Electrons are found in "shells" around a nucleus made up of protons and neutrons, positively charged and neutral particles (Figure 20). When the number of protons and electrons in an atom is equal, there is no net charge. When one outnumbers the other, the atom takes on either a positive or negative charge. Atoms of opposite charges attract; atoms of the same charge repel each other.

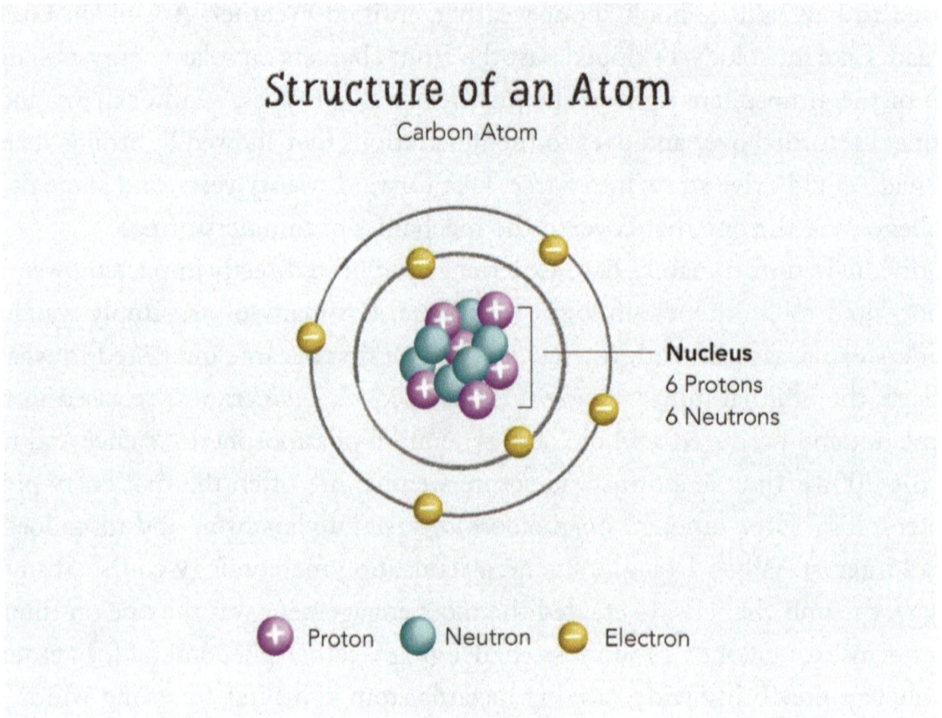

Figure 20

When objects of opposite charge are brought close together, the tendency is for electrons to "jump" across the air and neutralize the charge difference. The only problem is that air is an excellent insulator, which means that it is resistant to the flow of electrons. If the two objects are very far away, static electricity cannot be discharged—thus when your hand is very far away from the doorknob, you will not see a dramatic spark spreading across the room between your finger and the door. Additionally, if the magnitude of the charges is weak, there similarly will be no spark. In thunderstorm clouds, the vertical movement and interaction of liquid raindrops, ice crystals, and hailstones is thought to create areas of differing charge within a cloud. The top of the cloud has a generally positive charge, while the bottom of the cloud is generally negatively charged. The ground under the storm usually has a weak positive charge, because like charges repel and electrons are driven away from this area of the ground. When the difference in charge between the cloud (negative) and the ground (positive) becomes large enough to overcome the insulating properties of air, a lightning strike discharges between the cloud and the ground. Lightning bolts tend to strike the tallest nearby object first; this is why it is important to stay far away from trees and telephone poles if you are caught outside in a thunderstorm.

If lightning is caused by separation of charge in a cloud due to vertical motions of liquid water droplets and ice crystals, a logical conclusion is that thunderstorms must be the most efficient of all clouds at moving air up and down in the vertical; otherwise, all clouds would produce lightning. In fact, it is true that the most vigorous vertical motions (upward and downward) in the atmosphere are found in cumulonimbus, or thunderstorm clouds. These clouds can span the entire depth of the troposphere, and the air can be moving upward at over 100 miles per hour in some thunderstorms (52)! Recall from our stability discussion of the ball on the hill, the most unstable situation occurs when the ball is nudged down a very steep hill. In this case, the ball will rapidly accelerate in the direction of the initial push. Similarly, thunderstorms form in very unstable environments, where the air inside the cloud is much warmer than its surroundings and is very buoyant. These air parcels accelerate upward in much the same manner that the ball in our gravitational analogy will zip down the hill. Regardless of how the air is initially forced to rise (due to a front or a mountain range, for example), air parcels in an unstable environment will continue to accelerate upward until they hit the stratosphere or some other similarly stable layer in the atmosphere. This rising column of air is known as an updraft. When the air hits the stratosphere, it can no longer rise, as this area is very stable. The air spreads out horizontally, far away from the parent updraft, and produces the characteristic anvil cloud, which is often a harbinger of an incoming thunderstorm (Photo 14). In a well-developed thunderstorm, lightning can even occur between the high anvil cloud and the ground. These strikes are often deadly as people who were outdoors on a golf course, at a ball field, or on a hike will recollect that there was no rain or storm occurring at the time of the lightning strike.

Photo 14: Anvil cloud at the top of a thunderstorm. Image courtesy: NOAA/National Weather Service.

Life Cycle of a Thunderstorm

All thunderstorms move through a three-phase life cycle: phase one is primarily comprised of updrafts, phase two is comprised of both updrafts and downdrafts, and the final phase is dominated by downdrafts (Figure 21). During the updraft, or cumulus stage of development, unstable air is moving upward and precipitation-generation processes are beginning. Once precipitation particles become large enough such that the updraft is no longer able to keep them suspended, they begin to fall downward due to gravity and a downdraft develops.

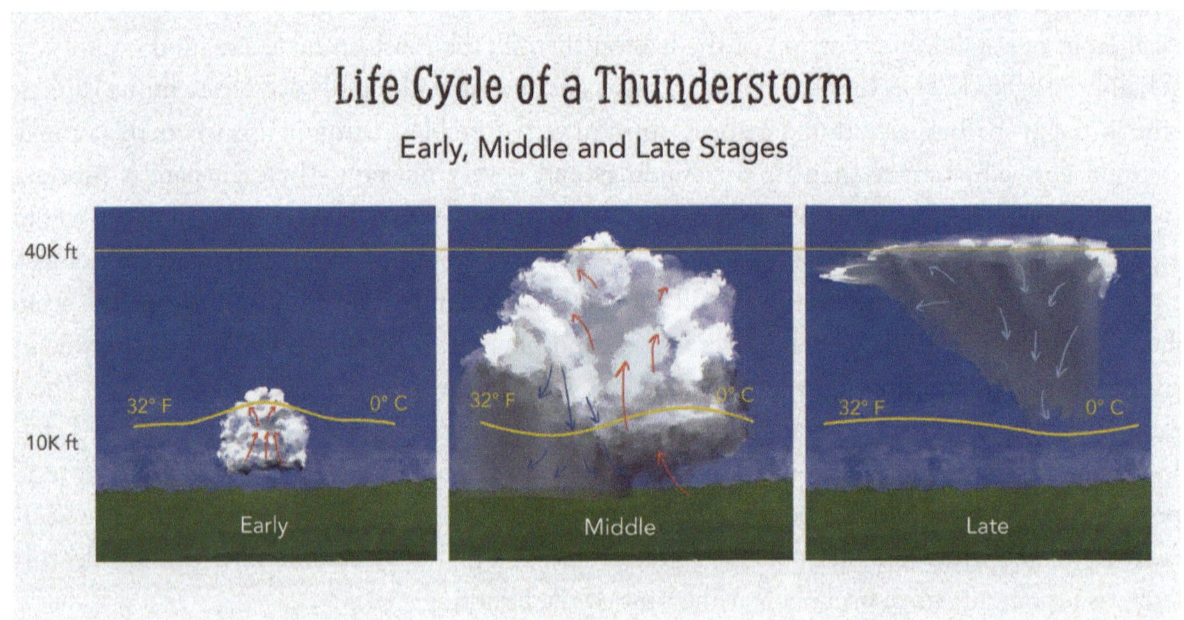

Figure 21

The storm is now in the middle phase of its life cycle. Evaporation of some of the particles cools the air in the downdraft column, which then becomes colder than the air around it. This negative buoyancy causes the air to accelerate downward, similar to the means by which air that is warmer than its environment will accelerate upward. The downdraft speeds downward, hits the ground and spreads out like pancake batter on a griddle. During this middle phase of development, the storm is at its most intense and contains both warm updrafts and cold downdrafts. This phase of the life of a thunderstorm may last anywhere from 30 minutes to several hours. If the air between the cloud and the ground is near saturation, precipitation will reach the ground in the form of rain or hail of varying intensity. In the late, or dissipating, stage of a thunderstorm, the storm no longer has a warm updraft and thus it begins to die off. Sometimes the storm is self-limiting, as the cold downdrafts "kill off" the updrafts. There may be lingering light precipitation during this last phase of thunderstorm development, but it tends to be much less intense than during the mature phase.

Ingredients for Thunderstorm Formation

At any given moment, there are around 2,000 thunderstorms occurring on Earth. What causes thunderstorms to form on some days, in some places, and not others? Thunderstorm formation is dependent on three primary criteria: rising air, atmospheric instability, and sufficient levels of moisture. Organized, long-lived thunderstorms that produce damaging winds, hail, or tornadoes need additional "ingredients." Let's look at each of these.

Rising air is essential to the formation of any cloud, including a thunderstorm cloud. Rising air cools, and cooling air brings it closer to the saturation point. If the air is sinking, or not rising high enough to reach its saturation point, no cloud will form. Thus, forecasters look for *lifting mechanisms*, or ways in which air is forced to rise. Examples of lifting mechanisms include mountains (orographic lift) and fronts, which are narrow areas of temperature contrast where cold, dense air forces warmer air upward. Sometimes air parcels become buoyant simply by becoming warmer than the air around them—think of a hot-air balloon rising from buoyancy, or the fact that the air inside the balloon is warmer and less dense than the air around it. Although thunderstorms can form simply from local buoyancy differences, many times there is some other lifting mechanism, such as a front, that helps to organize thunderstorms into a line or complex.

Instability is the second necessary ingredient for thunderstorm formation. We have previously talked about the concept of atmospheric stability, and how that relates to cloud formation. Thunderstorm clouds are vertically developed, meaning they have a fairly low base and extend all the way up to the top of the troposphere. In order to get air from the surface up to this altitude, the clouds need more than just a lifting mechanism located right near the surface. Recall that, in an unstable environment, air that is pushed upward by a lifting mechanism is warmer than the air around it, and will continue to accelerate off in the direction of the (upward) push. The greater the instability, the greater the upward acceleration. Thus, cumulonimbus clouds of great vertical depth can only occur in unstable environments; clouds in a stable environment tend to remain much shallower in depth.

Finally, forecasters look for the presence of low-level moisture as a necessary ingredient for thunderstorm formation. When low-level air is very dry, the cloud base tends to be very high. High-base thunderstorms can and do occur in areas such as the Rocky Mountains, but it is generally favorable to have ample moisture concentrated near the surface. This allows the cloud base to remain low to the ground, and as the second phase of the life cycle begins, allows precipitation to reach the ground rather than evaporating in the dry air underneath cloud base.

Types of Thunderstorms

When these three ingredients meet sufficient criteria, *ordinary cell thunderstorms* develop. Ordinary cell thunderstorms tend to be short-lived, moving through their life cycle in an hour or two.

While they can produce lightning and heavy rainfall, ordinary cell thunderstorms usually don't produce severe weather in the form of damaging wind gusts, large hail, or tornadoes. These types of thunderstorms form on a near-daily basis over the Florida peninsula, forcing theme park visitors, golfers, and tourists to run for cover until the storm passes.

In situations where the lifting mechanism is in the form of a front associated with an organized storm system, *multicell thunderstorms* develop. Multicell thunderstorms are groups of thunderstorms that are in various phases of their life cycle. These systems tend to form in areas that not only contain sufficient lift, instability, and moisture, but also have relatively strong vertical wind shear. Wind shear is simply the change in wind speed or direction with altitude. In the middle of a high-pressure system, winds tend to be weak from the surface all the way up through the troposphere. Thus, vertical wind shear is also relatively weak. In the vicinity of fronts, both wind speed and wind direction can change very rapidly with increasing altitude. This strong wind shear causes the thunderstorm updraft to tilt off the vertical, allowing the downdraft to form near, but not on top of, the updraft. Separating the updraft and downdraft allows for much longer-lived thunderstorms, which have ample time to develop and produce severe weather. Even multicell thunderstorms that are not producing severe weather can produce visually striking phenomena such as roll clouds, shelf clouds, and overshooting tops (Photo 15).

The Storm Prediction Center, the National Weather Service agency that is responsible for producing national outlooks and forecasts for severe thunderstorms, defines a severe thunderstorm as having any one of the following:

- Straight-line winds of at least 58 miles per hour (50 knots)
- Hail of at least one inch in diameter
- A tornado

While some severe thunderstorms produce only one of these types of weather, many severe thunderstorms produce multiple hazards. Damaging straight-line winds can occur in a thunderstorm when a fast-moving downdraft hits the ground and spreads out, and can cause as much damage as a low-end tornado. Meteorologists conduct damage surveys after a thunderstorm event to examine the pattern of damage and determine if it was produced by straight-line winds or the rotating winds of a tornado.

Sometimes, an intense thunderstorm downdraft will produce a *microburst*: a very narrow column of downward-moving air that is only about 2.5 miles across. A microburst can hit the ground and create extremely damaging winds at the surface, knocking down trees in all directions. It can also cause wind speeds of up to or over 100 miles per hour; the same as what can be found in a moderately intense hurricane (53)! Microbursts can be wet (accompanied by heavy precipitation), or dry, in cases where the precipitation evaporates before the microburst reaches the ground.

When a line of thunderstorms forms along or just ahead of a cold front, the storms can develop

Photo 15: Sunrise with a wall cloud moving over. Image courtesy: Mike Bodholdt/NOAA Photo Library. Bottom: Gust front "shelf cloud" on the leading edge of a complex of thunderstorms which produced a derecho. Image courtesy: Britney Misialek/NOAA Storm Prediction Center.

into an organized line that can extend hundreds of miles. *Squall lines*, or organized lines of thunderstorms, rely on lifting along a linear boundary, or front, to initiate, but then take on a life cycle of their own and can move away from the cold front (54). Within a squall line, individual thunderstorms are continually forming, developing, and ending their life cycle, allowing the squall line to persist for many hours. Sometimes the squall line will contain *bow echo* or *bowing line* segments (Photo 16), which can bring localized, damaging winds. The bow echo is so named because of the curved shape of the precipitation pattern that can be seen on radar: think of drawing an arrow in a bow, with the bow taking on a curved shape.

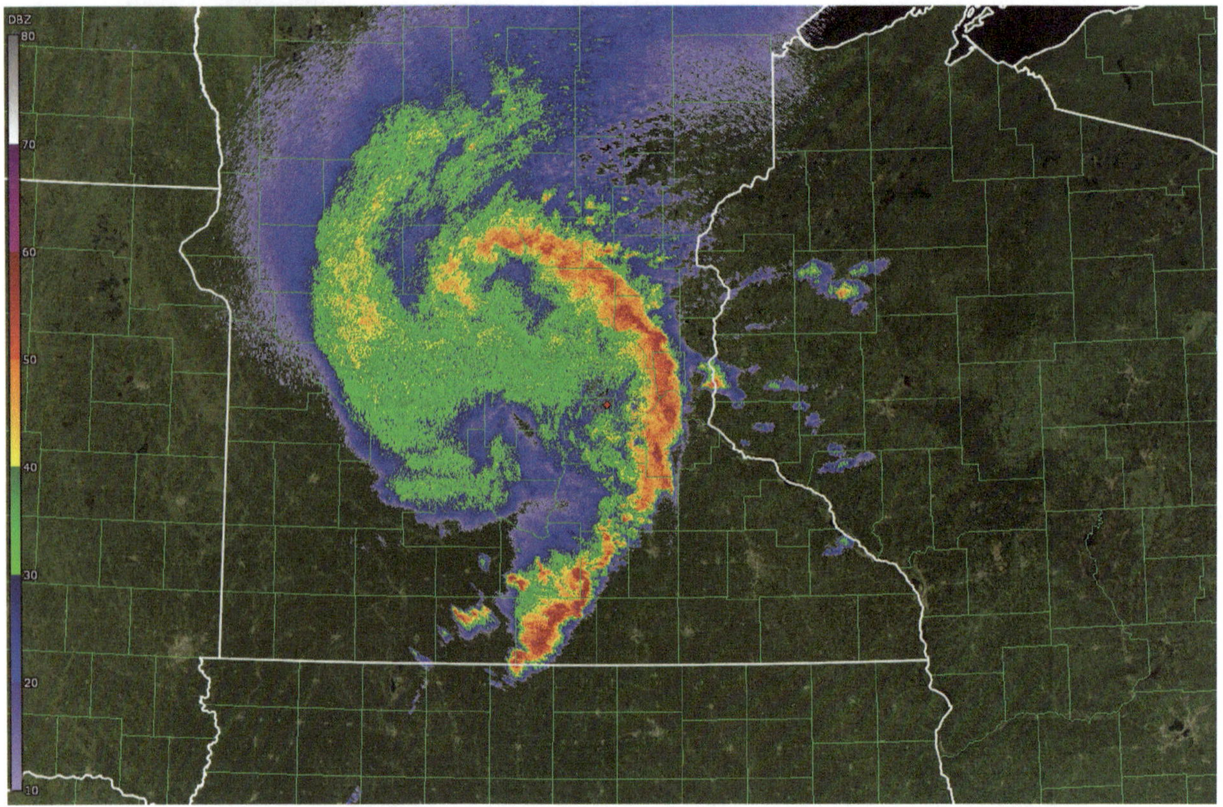

Photo 16: A bow echo seen on radar (May 11, 2022).

If the wind shear is just right, a squall line may be made up of a line of individual supercells, or rotating thunderstorms, which can produce tornadoes. Sometimes, linearly organized thunderstorms can form a *derecho* (55). A derecho is an exceptionally widespread, long-lived wind storm associated with a band of rapidly moving showers or thunderstorms, or squall line. Once formed, a derecho can last for many hours, and some derechos have brought widespread damaging winds across several states.

All About Derechos

While most people have heard of weather phenomena such as tornadoes and hurricanes, derechos are a lesser-known type of windstorm. Derechos are long-lived, organized lines of thunderstorms that produce broad areas of straight-line wind damage. Specifically, the swath of wind damage must extend at least 400 miles in length, be at least 60 miles wide, and include wind gusts of at least 58 miles per hour along most of its length.

Derechos can produce wind gusts in excess of 100 miles per hour and can lead to vast areas of damage. The term comes from a Spanish word for "direct," or "straight ahead," which contrasts with the rotational winds produced by tornadoes. While all regions in the path of a derecho can see damaging winds, localized downbursts in individual thunderstorms within the system often break out; these are the features that cause the strongest wind gusts within the derecho. Derechos tend to be most frequent across the United States from May through August. They can impact any part of the country east of the Rockies.

I recall the July 15, 1995, early-morning derecho that impacted New York. The day before, July 14, the Albany Airport reported a record-high temperature of 99 degrees Fahrenheit. That evening, a large, bow-shaped area of thunderstorms developed and moved into New York State, producing copious lightning and damaging winds as the storm tracked eastward. In the Adirondack Mountains, extensive areas of trees were blown down. Approximately 900,000 acres of forest were damaged across the state, and more than 30 campers and hikers had to be evacuated by helicopter because of downed trees blocking trails. Syracuse and Albany recorded wind gusts over 75 miles per hour as the derecho passed through. While we were lucky not to see any major damage at my house, I will never forget the nearly constant lightning!

More recently, derechos have impacted areas of the Midwest, Mid-Atlantic, and Great Lakes regions nearly every year in the spring and summer. Despite advance warning, these events often produce a great deal of damage, power outages, and sometimes injuries and fatalities, simply because of their large size and long life span (55).

Thunderstorms can also be organized into nonlinear systems, which are known as *mesoscale convective complexes* (MCCs). These systems of thunderstorms can be much larger than any single thunderstorm, and as large as the state of Iowa. As in the case of squall lines, these groups of thunderstorms work cohesively to create a very long-lived system; MCCs can last for more than twelve hours! MCCs tend to form during the summer months on the periphery of high-pressure areas, where the wind shear is relatively weak (56). MCCs are nocturnal in nature, forming during the late afternoon and peaking in intensity during the overnight hours. Although there is not always severe weather with these systems, they often produce incredible lightning displays and very heavy rainfall. Some of the biggest widespread flooding events in the Midwest are due to repeated MCCs crossing over a particular area or watershed. Often, an MCC will leave behind a remnant circulation, which acts as a trigger for thunderstorms, and development of a new MCC, the next day.

MCCs and Flooding: The 1993 Midwest Floods

Flooding can happen anywhere, for a variety of reasons: heavy rainfall, a dam break or ice jam, snow melt, or even high tides or storm surge. When flooding occurs rapidly, it is known as flash flooding. When intense rainfall quickly covers one area, nearby rivers and streams can rise rapidly in response. The subsequent decrease in levels as the water recedes can also happen quickly.

As the water from thunderstorms or other heavy rainfall works its way through a watershed, mainstem rivers can experience flooding many days after the rainfall ends. This type of flooding can persist for many days or weeks, and can be exacerbated by continued rainfall. Such was the case with the Great Mississippi River Flood of 1993.

The underlying causes of the 1993 flooding can be traced as far back as the fall of 1992, when above-normal precipitation across the Midwest created wet soil conditions. Persistent rainfall during the spring and summer months of 1993 resulted in far-above-normal rainfall across the upper Midwest. Many states saw three-month rainfall totals of more than 12 inches between June and August—200 percent higher than normal. At the Cedar Rapids Airport in Iowa, more than 48 inches of rain fell between April 1 and September 1. Normal precipitation for that area and time period is just over 21 inches!

While there were a handful of individual days where daily rainfall exceeded four inches, the astronomical total rainfall was largely due to repeated and persistent episodes of light-to-moderate rainfall during the entire time period. When this kind of pattern occurs over a widespread geographic area, mainstem rivers rise and remain high for extended periods of time.

As the rainwater slowly made its way through the Mississippi River watershed, small streams, minor rivers, and mainstem rivers all overflowed. Flooding was so widespread that, at points, approximately 600 river forecast points were above flood stage at the same time. Some gauges on the Mississippi river were above flood stage for 100 to 200 days! Because of the flat terrain and persistent high river flow, towns and farmland in flood plains all over the watershed were devastated. Numerous private and public levee systems experienced failure during the summer, further exacerbating the misery. An estimated 50 people died as a result of the flooding, and approximately 400,000 acres over nine states were affected (57).

The final type of thunderstorm we will discuss generates a great deal of interest among meteorologists and non-meteorologists alike: *supercell thunderstorms*. Supercell thunderstorms are characterized by the presence of a rotating updraft. Imagine air rising upward as if following the spirals of a Slinky™; this is essentially what occurs in a supercell storm. Supercell storms tend to form in environments where there is a great deal of both wind speed shear and directional shear. This changing of wind direction with height is what allows the updraft to begin to rotate. The rotating updraft, known as a *mesocyclone*, is strongly rotating such that it is discernible to forecasters on radar (Photo 9). Although tornadoes tend to develop underneath mesocyclones, scientists believe that only about 20 percent of supercell thunderstorms actually produce a tornado on the ground (58).

Lightning

Every year, individuals all around the United States are killed by either direct or indirect lightning strikes (59). As one might expect, most of the lightning strike fatalities occur during the summer months of June, July, and August; however, lightning can occur at any time of the year, in any part of the country (60). The general rule of thumb is that if you can hear thunder, you are at risk of being struck by lightning (even if the storm is not producing rain where you are). There is no place that is 100 percent safe if you are caught outdoors during a thunderstorm. If you cannot get to an indoor or sheltered location, the National Weather Service recommends the following (61):

- Avoid open fields, the top of a hill, or a ridge top.
- Stay away from tall, isolated trees or other tall objects. If you are in a forest, stay near a lower stand of trees.
- If you are in a group, spread out to avoid the current traveling between group members.
- If you are camping in an open area, set up camp in a valley, ravine, or other low area. Remember, a tent offers NO protection from lighting.
- Stay away from water; wet items, such as ropes; and metal objects, such as fences and poles. Water and metal do not attract lightning but they are excellent conductors of electricity, carrying the current from a lightning flash over long distances.

Even if you are inside a building during a thunderstorm, lightning can still be a risk. Lightning can strike a building directly, or travel through metal wires and pipes which conduct electricity. Inside, the National Weather Service recommends these actions (62):

- Don't touch electrical equipment such as computers, TVs, or cords. You can use remote controls safely.
- Avoid plumbing. Do not wash your hands, take a shower, or wash dishes.

- Stay away from exterior windows and doors that might contain metal components leading from outside your home to the inside.
- Stay off of balconies and porches and out of open garages or carports.
- Do not lie on concrete floors or lean against concrete walls.
- Protect your pets: dog houses are not safe shelters. Dogs that are chained to trees or on metal runners are particularly vulnerable to lightning strikes.
- Protect your property: lightning generates electric surges that can damage electronic equipment some distance from the actual strike. Typical surge protectors will not protect equipment from a lightning strike. Do not unplug equipment during a thunderstorm, as there is a risk you could be struck.

If you are outside in your garden and you see lightning or hear thunder, head indoors immediately. In all likelihood, your garden plants are not the tallest objects around and thus will not be directly impacted by a lightning strike, but even a strike to a nearby tree or power line can create hazards for nearby humans. Wait until several minutes without lightning or thunder have passed before returning outdoors.

Tornadoes

Tornadoes can occur at any time of year or location. They tend to occur at the highest frequency in what is known as Tornado Alley; eastern Colorado, northern Texas, Oklahoma, Kansas, Missouri, and Nebraska, as well as parts of the Dakotas and the Midwest. The most common time for tornadoes in Tornado Alley is during March, April, and May. Cold air masses from Canada, combined with warm, humid air masses from the Gulf of Mexico and strong winds aloft can create vigorous low-pressure systems that can result in the development of intense thunderstorms that produce tornadoes. A secondary peak of tornado occurrence happens during the fall season for a similar reason, as large temperature contrasts and strong winds aloft create dynamic weather systems.

Another area where tornadoes occur with some frequency is along the Gulf Coast and across the Southeast. This is because the warm, humid air that sits over the Gulf of Mexico combined with strong systems moving across the Southeast, can cause intense thunderstorms, even in the winter.

Tornadoes are rated in intensity on what is known as the Fujita Scale, or F-Scale, named after the pioneering researcher from the University of Chicago, Dr. Ted Fujita. Originally based strictly on wind damage, the scale was updated in 2007 with the help of engineers and other professionals, to reflect the fact that various structures can see drastically different damage from the same wind speeds. Today, the scale is known as the Enhanced Fujita scale. The scale rates tornadoes from EF-0 (estimated winds gusts between 65 and 85 miles per hour) to EF-5 (estimated wind gusts over 200 miles per hour). Thanks to interdisciplinary research and work across many areas of science, architecture, communication, and engineering, better building codes and construction practices, along with public safety campaigns, have helped to decrease tornado-related fatalities in recent decades.

Flooding

Any thunderstorm, even those that do not have severe weather warnings associated with them, can produce sudden downpours and flooding. During heavy downpours, flash flooding can cause water to pond across roadways, and that water often moves downhill at a rapid clip. Moving water, even just 12 inches deep, is strong enough to carry away a small car, but even large cars are susceptible to currents if water is deeper than 18 inches. The general rule of thumb is never to drive through a flooded roadway if you are not sure how deep the water is; it is possible that floodwaters could have washed the roadway away!

The National Weather Service issues several categories of flood statements. A Flood Watch means that flooding could occur, and preparations should be taken. Flood Advisories are issued for common or nuisance flooding, which has impacts on the environment but will not threaten life or property. Flood Warnings and Flash Flood Warnings are issued when flooding is imminent or underway. Flash flooding can occur anywhere at any time where heavy or persistent rainfall is occurring or where water levels rise and fall rapidly. Flood Warnings are generally issued as the wider river and stream network responds to rainfall, and thus usually affect areas in the immediate vicinity of mainstem rivers and streams. Flood Warnings can persist for days as river levels can remain high well after a heavy rainfall or rapid snow melt occurs.

In the garden, even a moderate amount of rainfall from a summer thunderstorm can briefly overwhelm raised beds and poorly drained areas. In forested areas, the tree canopy actually helps to impede the progress of heavy rainfall as it falls downward, thus helping to prevent temporary flooding during heavy rains. If you have a few large trees on your property, you likely have noticed this effect: the ground under the trees is the last to get wet at the start of a thunderstorm, and often it is possible to hear raindrops falling from the trees long after the storm has passed. One thing which you can do to mitigate the effects of brief downpours is to pay attention to the weather forecast when planning your watering schedule. Although a timer can be very convenient, especially when you are traveling, allowing your watering system to run sometimes is not necessary when thunderstorms are in the forecast. A thunderstorm can easily produce upwards of one half inch of rainfall in a short period of time. There are even 'smart' sprinklers on the market now which use weather networks to monitor weather conditions and adjust watering accordingly!

In order to plan your watering around the weather, it is important to know both how much rain is falling from the sky, as well as how much water is given to your garden via your irrigation system (whether you use sprinklers, drip irrigation, or another method). Installing a rain gauge on your property and taking regular measurements tells you how much natural water is entering your garden. Drip irrigation systems often tell you with the package information what the flow rate is, either in gallons per minute (GPM) or gallons per hour (GPH). If you water with a hose, simply water with the nozzle you usually use into a bucket for one minute and measure it using a large measuring cup; this is your GPM. Multiply this number by 60 to calculate your GPH. According to the U.S. Geological Survey, one inch of rainfall equates to six gallons of water per square yard. So, if you usually water your one square yard garden plot six gallons on a particular day, but you receive one half inch of rainfall, you would only need to water three gallons to supplement the natural rainwater and ensure your garden receives the appropriate amount.

Severe Weather, Thunderstorm Safety, and Your Garden

Although organized systems such as multicell and supercell thunderstorms are often expected to produce severe weather, any thunderstorm, even an ordinary cell thunderstorm, has the potential to produce dangerous conditions and/or severe weather. For example, any thunderstorm with cloud-to-ground lightning has the potential to become deadly. Additionally, ordinary cell thunderstorms sometimes form in areas where the steering winds are relatively weak. This means that storms can be slow to move, and thus can result in flash flooding. Thunderstorms can often create hazardous or severe weather very quickly. Knowing how to respond ahead of time can save both lives and property.

If you are outdoors gardening and thunderstorms are in the forecast, be aware of your surroundings. If you hear thunder, go inside and wait until at least 30 minutes have passed since the last rumble before going back outside. Even non-severe gusty winds with thunderstorms can knock over patio plants, so if there are any you are worried about you can bring those indoors if you know thunderstorms are in the forecast. As always, personal safety is paramount to saving any plants in the garden so be aware of the weather forecast if you plan to be outside.

Hurricane Basics

Hurricanes are storms that form as a result of weather disturbances in the tropical oceans, and can form in any ocean. Here in the United States, most hurricanes that impact the eastern half of the country form in the tropical Atlantic Ocean, while storms that impact the southwest United States generally form in the eastern Pacific. Tropical trade winds generally blow from the east to the west. In the Atlantic Ocean, most tropical disturbances originate off the equatorial African coastline and then move westward across the ocean. Depending on where you are located in the world, hurricanes may be called typhoons (western Pacific) or cyclones (Australia and India). The general term *tropical cyclone* refers to any area of low pressure that originates in the tropics and undergoes development or strengthening.

In the larger Pacific Ocean, hurricanes can form at any time of year. In the Atlantic Basin, the official hurricane season, as defined by the National Hurricane Center, runs from June through November. Hurricanes are more similar in scale to a low-pressure system that forms in the middle latitudes (we will discuss these in more detail in Chapter 4) than they are to individual thunderstorms, which may only be a few miles across.

Because they form in the tropics, hurricanes tend to have the warmest air located at the center of the storm. As a hurricane forms and moves through its life cycle, all while moving northward in an ocean basin, it is possible for colder air to be drawn into the storm. The storm then undergoes *extratropical transition*. Sometimes a storm can be stronger once it transitions into an extratropical storm; the name simply refers to the structure of the storm and where the colder and warmer air can be found. Just like all areas of low pressure, winds are governed by the pressure gradient and Coriolis forces, and so hurricanes that form in the Northern Hemisphere spin counterclockwise, while those that form in the Southern Hemisphere spin clockwise. As a result, hurricanes do not cross the equator.

When a weather disturbance or area of thunderstorms in the tropics begins to organize and the pressure lowers, the area will initially become known as a tropical depression, and receive a number assignment (numbers reset each season). Once the wind speeds reach 39 miles per hour, the storm is known as a tropical storm, and it receives a name. Atlantic storms have been named since 1953, and the names of storms around the world are now governed by the WMO. Seasonal hurricane names for each ocean basin are set by the WMO and there is a six-year rotation of names. Names for each season start with the letter A and move through the alphabet, alternating male and female names. If a storm is particularly impactful (such as hurricanes Sandy, Katrina, Harvey, and Ida) the name will be retired and not used in the future. Each named storm keeps its name for its entire life cycle, whether it strengthens or weakens or becomes extratropical.

Life Cycle of a Hurricane

After a tropical depression becomes a named tropical storm, it may undergo further strengthening, or it may dissipate over time. Once the winds reach 74 miles per hour, the storm becomes known as a hurricane. Hurricane strength is rated based on the Saffir-Simpson scale, which is analogous to the Fujita scale for tornadoes. The Saffir-Simpson scale was developed by engineer Herb Saffir and meteorologist Bob Simpson in the 1970s. The categories, from 1 to 5, are based on the maximum sustained wind speeds in a storm. The Saffir-Simpson scale does not specifically address all possible hurricane impacts, including heavy rainfall and storm surge (although storm surge is partially related to wind speed).

Hurricane Harvey (2017): Extreme Flooding

On August 25, 2017, Hurricane Harvey made landfall along the coast of Texas near Corpus Christi as a catastrophic Category 4 storm. Harvey grew in strength and size over the warm waters of the Gulf of Mexico. After landfall, the center of the storm stalled southeast of San Antonio, and eventually backtracked into the coastal waters south of Houston before again making landfall, this time as a tropical storm, just to the west of Lake Charles, Louisiana.

In addition to the direct impacts of a Category 4 hurricane, coastal Texas was subjected to extreme rainfall in the period after landfall, which resulted in catastrophic flooding. At Houston's William P. Hobby Airport, daily rainfall records were set each day between August 26 and August 28: 12.07 inches, 10.99 inches, and 9.41 inches, respectively. It became the wettest three-day period on record at the airport dating back to August 1930.

The top three, and five of the top ten, wettest three-day periods at the Houston Airport all occurred during Hurricane Harvey. A United States Geological Survey (USGS) hydrological gauge at Nederland, Texas, reported 60.58 inches of total rainfall, which set a North American record for rainfall from a tropical cyclone. The previous record (52 inches) was set by Hurricane Hiki in August 1950.

As a result of the slow-moving track, Harvey brought widespread, devastating impacts to large areas of Texas and Louisiana. At the time of this writing, the Insurance Information Institute ranks Hurricane Harvey as the fifth-costliest hurricane on record to impact the United States (63).

Hurricanes derive their energy from the warm oceans, so a necessary ingredient for hurricane formation is warm ocean water—generally around 80 degrees Fahrenheit (64). In order to start rotating, there has to be at least a weak Coriolis force, which is why hurricanes do not form directly on the equator. The final ingredient that allows hurricanes to develop into massive storms is weak wind shear. Weak wind shear and a deep layer of weak winds allow the heat released from thunderstorm clouds to remain at the center of the circulation, which then allows the pressure to fall at the center of the storm. That lowered pressure draws in more warm, humid air from the ocean to the storm center, allowing for further development. A hurricane will weaken and/or die out if any of the necessary ingredients are not available. For example, when a hurricane moves northward over cooler ocean waters or makes landfall and loses its source of warm ocean water altogether, it will weaken. If a hurricane moves into an area where upper-level winds are strong and wind shear becomes too great, it will likewise weaken.

------ *Hurricane Strength and Ocean Temperature* ------

Tropical systems, some of which become named tropical storms and hurricanes, derive their energy from warm ocean water. Scientific research has long documented the fact that the potential intensity at which storms can develop is related to the ocean temperature, up to a "maximum potential intensity" (65).

A 2020 study examined nearly 40 years of satellite data to quantify the link between increasing ocean temperatures and increases in tropical cyclone intensity. Researchers found a 15 percent increase in major (Category 3 or higher) hurricanes over the period from 1979 to 2017, which occurred in conjunction with a measurable increase in ocean temperatures in regions where tropical cyclones track.

The study noted that while there is a documented connection between increased sea surface temperatures and tropical cyclone intensity, numerous other factors can impact the strength of tropical systems, and thus it is not possible to quantify how much of the observed increase in intensity is due to human-induced climate change (66).

Once a storm becomes a hurricane, it has three main features. The center of the storm is known as the *eye*, which is characterized either by thin clouds, or even completely clear skies, and calm winds. The most intense part of the storm, where the strongest winds are found are in a ring around the eye, known as the *eye wall*. The heaviest precipitation is often found in the eye wall, as well. Outside of the eye wall are bands of thunderstorms, or *spiral rainbands*, which rotate around the storm center. Weak tornadoes can occur in the spiral rainbands, on the outskirts of a landfalling hurricane.

---------------- *Hurricane Hunters* ----------------

NOAA has a fleet of ten crewed aircraft and several drones that participate in hurricane observation and research, emergency response, and other operations to support science. "Hurricane Hunter" planes are a part of this fleet and are responsible for collecting data in both developing and mature tropical systems, to help forecasters better predict these storms.

Two Lockheed WP-3D (P3) Orion aircraft and one Gulfstream IV-SP (G-IV) can be used for Hurricane Hunter flights. Additionally, the U.S. Air Force Reserve's 53rd Weather Reconnaissance Squadron also participates in observations, using their WC-130J plane. The P3 aircraft fly missions that last up to ten hours, criss-crossing several times through a storm. Measurements are taken via onboard equipment (temperature, wind, humidity, and pressure sensors, and Doppler radar), as well as by GPS-guided dropsondes, or radiosondes that are dropped from the plane and take measurements as they sink toward the surface.

The G-IV plane has the ability to cruise as high as 45,000 feet, and thus can take upper-air observations near the top of developing storms. Outside of hurricane season, the NOAA fleet is used for taking measurements during winter storms, research projects, and high-impact atmospheric rivers that bring heavy rainfall to the West Coast. Despite the dangers of flying head-on into intense storms, NOAA Hurricane Hunters have an excellent safety record, and the pilots and crew have the skills and training necessary to keep all aboard safe in the most unfavorable flying conditions (67).

Figure 22

Hurricane Damage

While tornadoes tend to be a mile or less across, a hurricane can have impacts over an area hundreds of miles wide. A landfalling hurricane will tend to bring the strongest winds to the area on the right side of its direction of motion, or right-of-track (Figure 22). In addition to strong winds and heavy rainfall, the storm winds push ocean water onshore, creating a storm surge. The latter can be especially damaging to coastal locations when a storm makes landfall near the time of high tide. The rise of the water combined with its strong force can reduce coastal homes to rubble.

Heavy rains can also cause devastating inland flooding hundreds of miles away from the center of a hurricane, even after a storm makes landfall and has weakened. Warm, humid tropical air from the storm can be carried inland and forced to rise over hills and mountains. This is a particular problem for areas of the Northeast United States and the Appalachian Mountains, when an Atlantic storm makes landfall along the Eastern Seaboard or along the Gulf Coast.

Hurricanes Irene and Ida

Hurricanes Irene (2011) and Ida (2021) both had devastating impacts in the Northeastern United States. These storms are excellent examples of how hurricane impacts can extend well away from the point of landfall, and how even weak tropical systems can cause extreme devastation.

Hurricane Irene formed as an area of low pressure in the Atlantic Ocean and became a named tropical storm north of Barbados on August 21. The storm intensified to hurricane strength as it passed over Puerto Rico, hit the Bahamas as a Category 3 storm, and remained at hurricane strength as it moved northwest again and recurved east of the southeast United States.

Irene then tracked northward, making landfall in eastern North Carolina on August 27 as a Category 1 storm. As the storm continued to track northward, it gradually weakened to tropical storm strength as it moved over southern New Jersey. The center of Irene tracked over eastern New Jersey, western Connecticut and Massachusetts, and along the New Hampshire-Vermont border before becoming extratropical and continuing northward through western Maine and into Canada.

Irene brought peak winds between 65 and 70 miles per hour as it moved through New Jersey and the New York metropolitan area, although these winds remained well east of the center, sparing New York City from direct impact. However, the interaction of Irene with an upper-level disturbance allowed for heavy rainfall across Eastern New York and Western New England. Widespread rainfall of five to 10 inches occurred across the Catskill Mountains in New York, the Berkshire Hills in Massachusetts, and the Green and White mountains in Vermont and New Hampshire. Several long-term weather stations reported record or second-highest daily rainfall totals, including in Albany, New York, and Montpelier and Morrisville, Vermont. The rain caused widespread catastrophic flooding in these areas, destroying an estimated 2,400 roads, 800 homes and businesses, and 300 bridges (68). Many of the roads took years to rebuild. It is possible to drive through remote areas of Vermont today and still see damage caused by Hurricane Irene.

Hurricane Ida formed on August 26, 2021, near Kingston, Jamaica. The storm moved into the warm waters of the Gulf of Mexico and quickly strengthened to a Category 4 storm. It made landfall near Port Fourchon, Louisiana, on the morning of August 29 as a devastating Category 4 storm. After causing extensive impacts along the Gulf Coast, the storm weakened as it moved inland through northern Mississippi, Tennessee, West Virginia, and Maryland. Ida became known as an extratropical storm once it was located over West Virginia, and the storm continued to track to the northeast through Maryland and central New Jersey before continuing eastward to the south of Long Island.

Ida brought extreme rainfall, with rates above three inches per hour in some areas, to Eastern Pennsylvania, New York City, and the mid-Hudson Valley of New York, as well as southern Connecticut and Rhode Island. The automated sensor in New York's Central Park recorded 3.15 inches of rain in one hour, and several stations in the New York State Mesonet network located in the New York City metro area recorded rainfall rates of three to four inches per hour. This resulted in storm total rainfall amounts of eight to 10 inches in the swath where the heaviest rain fell. Newark International Airport in New Jersey and LaGuardia Airport in New York set all-time daily rainfall records on September 1, 2021: 8.41 inches and 6.80 inches, respectively. Several other stations saw rainfall totals in the top five for their period of record.

We often forget that Ida occurred on the heels of Tropical Storm Henri, which also brought heavy rainfall to the region just two weeks earlier. The National Weather Service issued several Flash Flood Emergency statements during the course of the storm; these statements are issued when extreme or life-threatening flooding is imminent or occurring. Prior to Ida, there had never been a Flash Flood Emergency issued for New York City.

Despite the warnings, the flooding resulted in stranded vehicles, extensive impacts to the subways and other public transportation, and vast damage to buildings and infrastructure. At least 48 people died in the Northeast. Thirteen of them were in New York City; many of these were residents of basements or low-level apartment buildings. Post-analysis of Ida resulted in a focus on better ways for the National Weather Service to communicate with local authorities and emergency managers to highlight the severity of extreme flooding occurring in conjunction with a weakening or post-tropical cyclone (69).

Generally speaking, if a hurricane is approaching your area (whether you are located inland or near the coast), you should assemble a disaster kit that includes food and water for at least three days, prescriptions and other medicines, first aid supplies, a battery-powered radio and flashlights, and some cash for necessary purchases in the event that power is not on at local stores. You can even assemble a disaster kit when a storm is not imminent so that it is ready to go at all times; just check it periodically to ensure that medications and food remain within their expiration dates. Ensuring everyone has a charged cell phone can be particularly helpful if family members are in separate locations. It is also important to have an emergency plan set up in advance, so that everyone knows what to do and where to meet up in the event of an emergency. Additionally, you can take steps in advance to prepare and protect property if needed. Follow the guidance of local and state officials for preparations, and stay aware of any mandatory or voluntary evacuations. As with many other weather hazards, if a Hurricane or Tropical Storm Watch is in effect, take preventive actions. Once they are upgraded to a Hurricane or Tropical Storm Warning, preparations should be complete, and weather conditions should be monitored carefully.

If you are a gardener and a hurricane is making its way towards your area, you likely will be most concerned with making sure your property is prepared for the impacts. However, you can also take some steps to prepare your garden as well. First, be sure to pay attention to the weather forecast to understand what the storm impacts are expected to be in your area. Many naturally occurring plants in coastal hurricane zones are built to withstand strong winds, but it is also a good idea to prune any loose or low-hanging branches in advance of a storm. As with any anticipated high winds, you will want to ensure that all of your tools are picked up and that any loose objects in your garden are stored away or secured. Also, take the time to pick any ripe or nearly-ripe fruits and vegetables, as they may fall to the ground during heavy rain and winds. If heavy rain is in your forecast, ceasing your normal watering schedule for a week or so prior may help to offset some of the excess. That being said, extreme rainfall that can sometimes occur with hurricanes and tropical storms may still damage shallow-rooted or weaker plants. As with any severe weather, your primary focus should be protecting people in advance of a hurricane.

Wrap-up: Summer

Summer gardening can be a wild, weather-dependent ride, courtesy of some of the most wild and dramatic weather that occurs on the planet in this season. Knowing what to do in advance of incoming hazardous weather can both save lives and protect your property. Be sure to review the safety tips we have discussed here on a seasonal basis to refresh your memory on what to do if severe weather comes your way.

Gardener Goals

- Download three different weather apps on your phone and spend some time learning about the features of each. Enable location services and learn what types of weather notifications are pushed to your phone.
- If you don't already, start tracking how much water you are putting into your garden with your routine watering schedule. Consider investing in a rain gauge and tracking daily precipitation in the same notebook. Make notes about the performance of various plants in your garden over the course of a growing season and think about how you might adjust your watering schedule based on the weather conditions.
- Review weather safety procedures for the weather hazards which are most common to your location. Although this is not specifically related to gardening, knowing what to do in an emergency or in advance of severe weather can save lives and prevent injuries.

Chapter 4

Autumn

Autumn Gardening: Cleaning up and Hunkering Down

Autumn, after summer, is one of the best times of year here in the Northeast. Even in years when the foliage is subpar, there are still beautiful colors to be found on bright, clear, autumn days. One of my favorite things to do is watch individual trees. There are a few maples along my usual travel routes that color very early in the fall, while others turn brilliant red and orange much later. Oak trees, which abound in my yard and the woods surrounding my neighborhood, turn an unimpressive brown and often keep some of their leaves even into March! The rose of Sharon in my yard is one of the last plants to bloom each summer, and can still produce flowers into September. The leaves of my astilbe, which grow on the shady side of my house, turn a brilliant red as they begin to go dormant, as do the leaves on the burning bush. (Photo 17).

In the vegetable garden, most years I continue to get tomatoes and green beans until the first frost. When I know a cold night is imminent, I usually pull the last of my green tomatoes and allow them to ripen right on my kitchen windowsill. I save seeds from all of my plants for use the following year. Additionally, because herbs are generally not cold-hardy, I will cut the stems of my patio herbs before the first frost and hang them upside down in my garage to dry, before crumbling them into jars for later use. Some people plant cold-season crops of vegetables such as lettuce and peas in the fall, for one more round of fresh vegetables before the winter. Although I often aspire to this, between my children's busy school schedules and the decreased daylight, there is precious little time for me to get outside and work in the garden.

After a killing frost has occurred, it is time to transport the fig tree to its winter home in my garage. It is also time to pull out the remaining plants in the vegetable garden and rake it out so it is all ready to refresh with compost in the spring. With all of the oak trees in my yard, autumn is a very busy time for raking and leaf blowing! Although I feel sad every year when I look at my empty garden beds, there is something gratifying about knowing they are all ready to go in the spring.

Photo 17: Some of my favorite garden snapshots from years past. Left to right, top to bottom: Purple crocuses are the first harbingers of spring; a rose plant which I discovered buried behind several large shrubs, which is very happy in its new location; pink astilbe are one of my favorite shade plants; hibiscus, with stunning dinner-plate-sized blooms; a birdbath full of shade-loving impatiens; echinacea (coneflower) in a unique 'wild berry' color; Shasta daisies in full bloom; a lovely hydrangea which was gifted to me; garden phlox, a relatively new favorite of mine; an assortment of perennials along a retaining wall which I add to yearly; the 'miracle' rose of Sharon in full bloom.

Autumn Topic #1: Optics

There are countless ways that atmospheric gasses, suspended particles, and light from the sun play together to create interesting features. We'll examine some of the more common optical phenomena. This chapter is by no means exhaustive, but I hope that you will remember seeing some of these in the past—or, better yet, look up and observe today, tomorrow, or in the future as you enjoy the outdoors in your garden.

Rainbows

Rainbows are one of nature's most colorful phenomena (Photo 18). The fact that they often appear in conjunction with the dark and stormy skies of thunderstorms makes them a symbol of hope for many cultures. Rainbows occur when visible light of all wavelengths is broken up into its component parts.

Photo 18: Primary (interior arc) and secondary (exterior arc, inverted colors) rainbows. Image courtesy: Mary Hollinger/NOAA Photo Library.

When visible light of all wavelengths travels intact together, we see white light. A process called refraction, or bending of light waves, allows white light to be broken up into each color on the EM spectrum. Refraction occurs when light crosses a boundary between two different densities—say, air and water. Refraction of the light is the reason why, when you step into a still clear pond or lake, your feet look different than they do when you step out of the water.

When light from the sun passes from the air into a rain droplet, refraction separates the light into its component colors. That refracted light is then reflected off the back of the raindrop, much like a mirror, and refracted again upon exit. When the light hits your eye, you see each color separately (Figure 23).

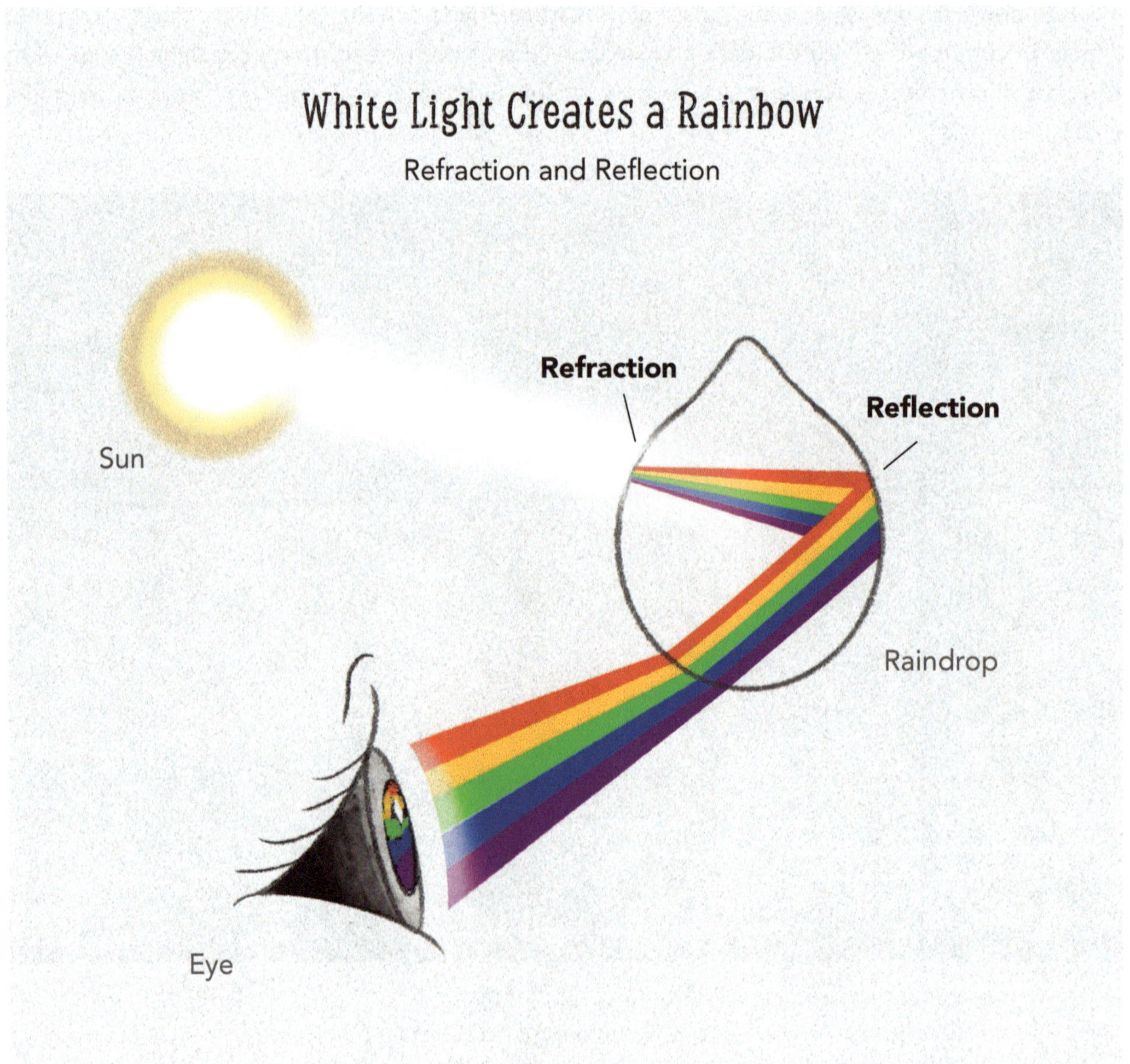

Figure 23

I had a small prism when I was a child. I loved to hold the prism up to a sunny window or shine a flashlight through it and see it form a rainbow on the floor in front of me. I didn't realize it at the time, but the same process of refraction that creates rainbows with light and raindrops is what was causing the rainbows on the floor with my prism. Air and glass have different densities, just like air and water, and so refraction of white light causes color separation to occur.

In order to see a rainbow, look for dark clouds ahead of you while the sun is at your back. Where I live, storms usually approach from the west, and when they pass through to the east in the late afternoon, the pre-setting sun in the western sky creates rainbows as I look to the east. I have also seen rainbows early in the morning after sunrise, as I look to the west for oncoming precipitation, with the sun in the east at my back.

Sometimes we see a double rainbow, or one arc outside the other. In this case, the inner arc has the traditional or more common arrangement of colors, with red on the outside and violet on the inside. The secondary rainbow is usually fainter, but always will have the colors reversed: red on the inside and violet on the outside. Secondary rainbows occur when the sun angle allows for not one, but two reflections off of the back of the raindrop before the separated light exits the drop.

A supernumerary rainbow, a very rare phenomenon, can occasionally be seen as well. I have only seen a supernumerary rainbow once in my life—and of course I didn't get a picture, because I had an ice cream cone in my hand! It was something I will not forget. Supernumerary rainbows are striking because they appear to be multiple rainbows stacked up together. These bows can be seen on the inside of a primary rainbow arc, or occasionally on the outside of a secondary arc. When light waves exiting many raindrops interfere with each other, a diffraction pattern can form, and a supernumerary rainbow appears. Think of it this way: when you drop a rock into a still pond, you see a pattern of waves emanating outward. When you drop two rocks near each other, a diffraction pattern appears as the waves from each rock interact with each other (Photo 19).

Photo 19: A diffraction pattern on the surface of a pond (image courtesy Maja R./Unsplash).

Green Flash

Green flash (Photo 20), like rainbows and many other optical phenomena, occurs because light from the sun is refracted, or bent, as it travels through the atmosphere. Recall that refraction occurs when light changes speeds as it moves through different mediums of different densities. In the case of rainbows, that happens when light travels from air into the liquid water of the raindrop. In the case of a green flash, the atmosphere itself is the cause of the refraction.

Photo 20: Green flash above the setting sun at Pigeon Point, California. Jan Null states: "A monster green flash at Pigeon Point like I have never seen before; it lasted nearly a minute." Image courtesy: Jan Null.

Air near the surface of the earth is much denser than air high up in the atmosphere. When it is near sunset and the sun is low on the horizon, the light has to pass through a long pathway of air of many different densities before it reaches your eye. As the sun starts to set below the horizon, the light that reaches your eye is refracted and broken up into its component colors. The yellow portion of the visible light spectrum can be seen near the top of the sun, and just above it appears the green. It is a very brief occurrence, hence the term 'green flash'; once the sun dips below the horizon, the phenomenon is gone. In fact, the blue and violet colors of the spectrum should be located above the green flash, but we cannot see them with our eyes because the blue and violet colors are preferentially scattered by atmospheric gasses, as we discussed in Chapter 1 when we covered sunsets.

Twilight

Twilight is simply the time of day at dawn or dusk when there is still visible light even though the sun is below the horizon. This phenomenon is yet another example of atmospheric refraction and scattering of visible light from the sun. As the sun dips very close to the horizon at sunset, refraction of its light through the atmosphere causes it to appear higher up in the sky than it actually is. This is, in essence, a mirage—a phenomenon which we will discuss shortly. Refraction, in

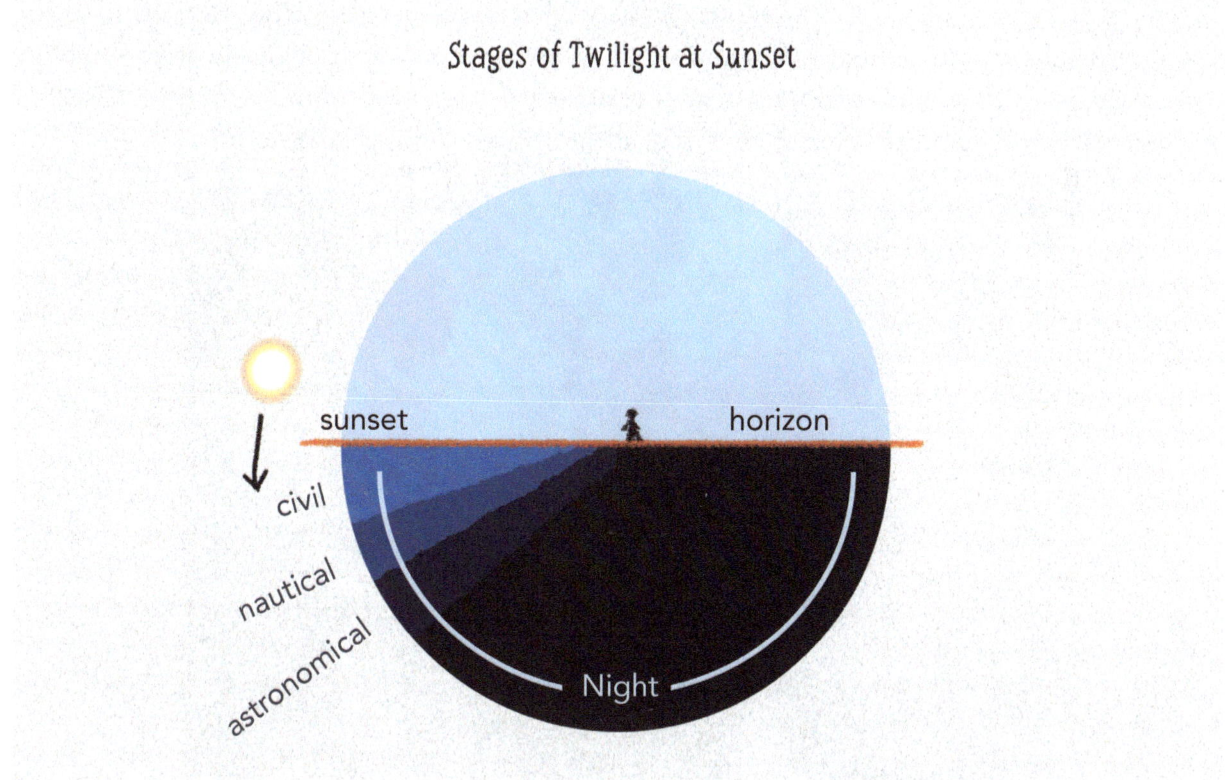

Figure 24

addition to scattering of sunlight by the Earth's atmosphere, prolongs daylight by several minutes on either end of the day.

There are three phases of twilight, each of which has an official definition based on how far below the horizon the center of the sun's disk is located (Figure 24). Each phase is progressively darker than the one before as the sun sets; at sunrise, the order of the phases is reversed as the sky gets progressively lighter. Let's consider sunset to illustrate this point. The initial phase of twilight occurs when the center of the disk lies between the horizon and six degrees below the horizon. During this phase, known as civil twilight, it is still light enough to do things such as putting your gardening tools away. When the sun is between 6 and 12 degrees below the horizon, it is nautical twilight, so named because mariners are not able to navigate by visuals alone, because it is not possible to see the horizon. The darkest phase of twilight, astronomical twilight, occurs when the sun is between 12 and 18 degrees below the horizon. During astronomical twilight, it is possible to see objects in the night sky, such as stars and planets, when light pollution from cities does not interfere. After the sun is 18 degrees below the horizon, it is officially night and the sky is totally dark.

Mirages

Mirages (Photo 21) are one of the coolest atmospheric phenomena I know of. If you have ever driven down the road on a hot summer day and seen "wobbles" just above the roadway off in the distance, you have seen a mirage. Mirages occur when light passes through air of very rapidly changing density. Thus, when a column of air is extremely hot at the bottom (like near the blacktop of a roadway in the summer), or extremely cold at the bottom, a mirage can occur.

Photo 21: Mirage over Cook Inlet, Alaska. Image courtesy: Commander George Leigh/NOAA Photo Library.

Superior Mirage
Superior Mirage
Warmer Air
Eye/brain construct a straight line path of received light
Path of Light
Cold Air
Actual Object
Observer

Inferior Mirage
Actual Object
Colder Air
Observer
Path of Light
Warm Air
Warm Surface
Eye/brain construct a straight line path of received light
Inferior Mirage

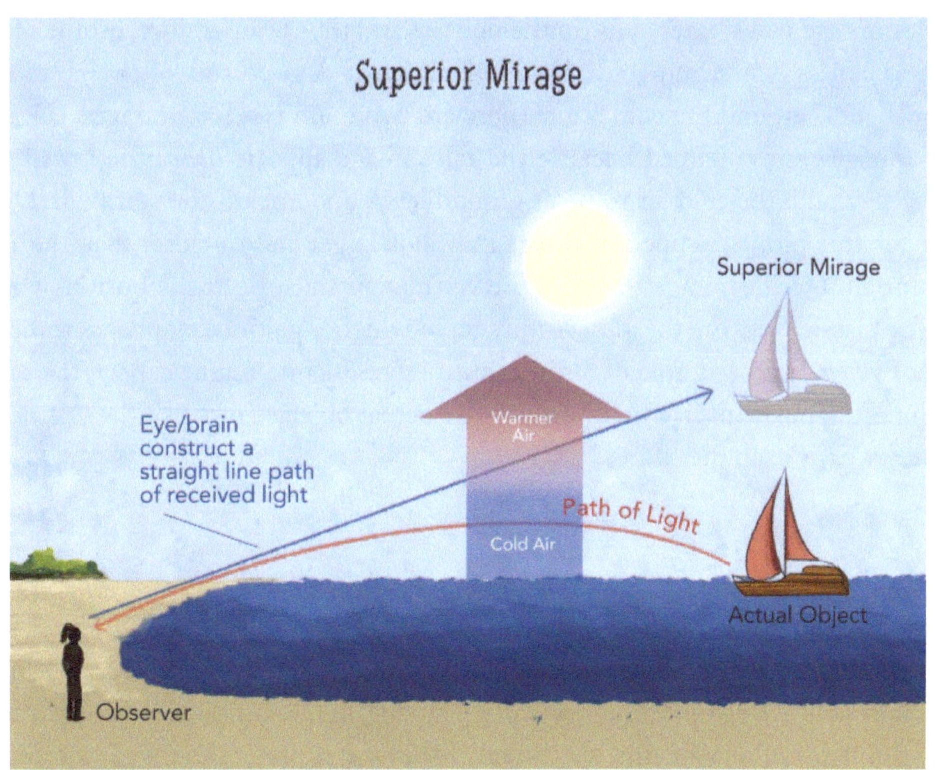

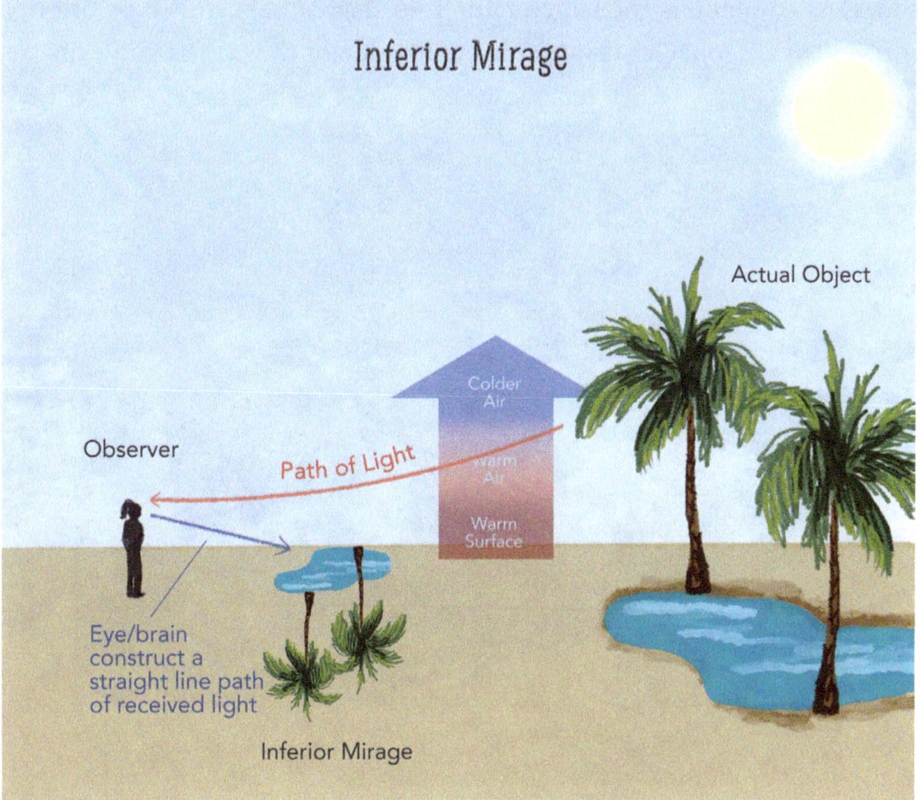

Figure 25

The type of mirage you see depends on the density, and thus temperature, profile of the air. Very hot air tends to be less dense, and colder air is more dense. A good rule of thumb to remember is that the light "bends" around the colder air. There are two main types of mirages. (Figure 25).

Superior mirages are so named because the false image appears *above* the actual object; these types of mirages require the cold air to be at ground level, underneath the warm air. Depending on the exact temperature profile, a superior mirage may look larger and/or closer than the actual object.

In order for an inferior mirage to occur, the warmer air must be at the bottom, with colder air on the top. The classic oasis-in-the-desert mirage, in which a palm tree appears to be reflected in a calm body of water, is an example of an inferior mirage. As one might expect, the false image of an inferior mirage appears inverted underneath the actual object—just like the upside down palm tree in our desert oasis example.

Halos, Sun Dogs, and Sun Pillars

A halo (Photo 22) is a ring or arc of bright light that surrounds the sun. In order for a halo to occur, there must be very high, thin cirrus clouds comprised of hexagonal ice crystals in front of the sun. These ice crystals act just like tiny prisms, refracting light as it passes through them. The refracted light through millions of tiny ice crystals focuses at a preferential spot located 22 degrees around the sun. Less common is the larger, fainter 46-degree halo. This type of bright arc occurs when light enters the hexagonal ice crystals through a side of the crystal and exits from the hexagon's base.

Photo 22: Halo surrounding the sun, April 2023. Image courtesy: Jan Null.

Depending on the situation, there may be sun dogs (Photo 23) at the same time as a halo, although this is not always the case. Sun dogs are bright spots that appear on either side of the sun. Sometimes there may be only one bright spot, if the cirrus cloud deck is broken in places. Sun dogs usually form because of plate-shaped, hexagonal ice crystals. These plate-shaped crystals tend to orient themselves horizontally, and thus the light passing through is preferentially refracted at specific locations, which is where the sun dogs appear. Some sun dogs appear to have many colors, similar to when light passes through a prism, although many sun dogs just appear as white bright spots.

Photo 23: Sun dogs to the left and right of the sun through a high cirrus cloud deck. Image courtesy: Sally Ortiz/NOAA Photo Library.

Photo 24: Sun pillar extending vertically above the setting sun. Image courtesy: Grand W. Goodge/NOAA Photo Library.

The final phenomenon that forms as a result of ice crystals in front of the sun is a sun pillar (Photo 24). As the name implies, these features appear as bright towers of light extending above and/or below the sun. It is typical to see sun pillars in the presence of fresh, white snow when the sun is low on the horizon. The millions of tiny ice crystals that make up cirrus clouds can also act like tiny mirrors that reflect light, in addition to refracting light. As with sun dogs, sun pillars generally form when the ice crystals are horizontally oriented six-sided plates, which is the best configuration for them to behave as tiny mirrors and reflect light upward or downward. At certain times, all three of these phenomena may appear together in the sky.

Coronas, Glories, and Crepuscular Rays

Earlier in this chapter we discussed that diffraction occurs when waves create an interference pattern. Because light travels as waves, diffraction patterns can form when light passes around obstacles. Both coronas and glories form as a result of diffraction of light.

While they can form around the sun, coronas (Photo 25) are more commonly observed surrounding the moon, because it is easier to see around a dimmer planetary body. When a thin cloud is made up of tiny liquid cloud droplets (which are much smaller than the raindrops that create rainbows), these droplets create an interference pattern as the moonlight passes through the cloud. Coronas appear to be almost prismatic, colorful concentric rings of light around the moon. These features can sometimes be confused with halos, but they do not form under the same conditions.

Photo 25: Corona around the moon. Photo Courtesy: Lourdes Avilés.

Photo 26: Glory surrounding the shadow of a NOAA Twin Otter aircraft projected onto a low cloud deck. Image courtesy: LCDR Phil Hall/NOAA Photo Library.

Glories (Photo 26) are some of the most interesting phenomena you can observe, if you are lucky enough to catch one. I have seen glories occasionally when I have been in an airplane that was flying above a low cloud deck. In other words, where the plane was flying above the clouds it was sunny, and I was looking down at the thick clouds below. Just as when moonlight passes through a cloud and a diffraction pattern forms, the same thing happens when sunlight interacts with the clouds below the airplane. A glory appears as a colorful ring around the shadow of the plane which is cast on the clouds from the sun above.

Crepuscular rays (Photo 27) are a stunning optical phenomenon in which visible rays appear to emanate outward from the sun, generally near sunrise or sunset. Although the rays appear to diverge away from each other due to our perspective from Earth, they are actually parallel! Crepuscular rays can be seen when the sun is partially blocked by a cloud that allows sunbeams to pass through small gaps in the cloud. Dust and haze in the atmosphere can help make crepuscular rays even more visible.

Photo 27: Crepuscular rays. Image courtesy: Grand W. Goodge/NOAA Photo Library.

Autumn Topic #2: Precipitation Types

We have discussed many aspects of saturation, humidity, and condensation, and now it is time to put it all together and talk about what we all experience here on the ground: precipitation. Even if you live in a warm climate where most precipitation falls as rain, you may have experienced other types of precipitation, such as hail during a thunderstorm. If you live in a colder climate, you likely have observed that frozen precipitation can take many different forms.

In meteorology, there are three categories of observable weather phenomena: precipitation, obscurations to visibility, and "other" phenomena. We have already discussed fog and mist, which are obscurations to visibility. Smoke, dust, sand, and even volcanic ash are other types of particles in the atmosphere that may reduce visibility, so they are also considered obscurations. "Other" phenomena include things that do not fit neatly into the precipitation or obscurations categories, and include features such as dust devils, tornadoes, funnel clouds, and dust storms.

In order to be classified as precipitation, the particles must be falling from the atmosphere and reaching the ground. Cloud droplets, as we have discussed, are so tiny that they are able to remain suspended in the air. Once these cloud droplets (or ice crystals) grow to a large enough size, they begin to fall downward due to the Earth's gravity. If the particles do not completely evaporate on their journey downward to Earth, they are called precipitation.

What type of precipitation hits the ground (or your head, should you be caught outdoors without an umbrella) is determined by the temperature profile between ground level and the cloud base from which the particles are falling (70). Although it seems counterintuitive, much of the precipitation that falls, even during summer thunderstorms, initially forms in the cloud as ice crystals, because the temperature inside the cloud is generally below freezing. In very tall thunderstorms, the lower portions of the cloud can sometimes be above freezing, so some precipitation can form as liquid raindrops as well (see the discussion on thunderstorms and lightning in Chapter 3).

Here, we will use the word *warm* to mean above-freezing temperatures, and *cold* to mean below-freezing. Even though temperatures in the 40s Fahrenheit may not feel warm, they are well above the freezing point, which is crucial in our discussion about how precipitation forms.

In the summer, there is a deep layer of warm air between the ground and cloud base, which may be up to 10,000 feet in altitude. Thus, any precipitation that forms as ice crystals (snow) inside the cloud has ample time to melt as it falls to the ground. Precipitation that hits the ground in liquid form is known either as rain or drizzle. Rain has a larger drop size (technically speaking, at least 0.02 inches in diameter), while drizzle is made up of very tiny drops that are still large enough to fall to the ground. Sometimes, drizzle can be very difficult to distinguish from mist or fog! Even in winter storms, if there is a deep enough layer of above-freezing air, precipitation will melt as it travels to the ground and result in rainfall instead of snow. Conversely, when the air column is entirely below freezing, precipitation remains all snow. This is the simplest scenario: the precipitation forms in a cold cloud as ice crystals, which then fall through a layer of air that is completely below the freezing point from cloud base down to the ground.

Even within this single precipitation type, there are numerous variations of how the snow can look. William "Snowflake" Bentley was a Vermont native who pioneered the field of photomicrography, or taking photographs of very tiny things through a microscope (71). He famously photographed more than 5,000 snow crystals, which were studied in the decades to follow. Dr. Kenneth Libbrecht of the California Institute of Technology has extensively studied the physics of ice crystal growth, and maintains the website snowcrystals.com. Here, you can learn the details of how snowflakes form and explore galleries of numerous types of snowflakes. Snowflakes can take on many shapes, depending on the temperature of the environment in which they form (72). Dendrites are the six-sided shapes that most people first think of when they hear the word *snowflake*. Snow can also take the form of six-sided columns, needles, six-sided plates, and many other shapes.

Where things really get interesting, at least in terms of precipitation type, is when the layer between the cloud and the ground is not entirely above freezing (Figure 26). Precipitation falls as either sleet or freezing rain in the in-between areas, where there is some warm air underneath the cloud, but not enough to allow for plain rain. Sleet occurs when there is ample warm air just underneath the cloud base that allows precipitation to partially or fully melt as it falls toward the ground. However,

Figure 26

underneath lies a deep layer of cold air. As the drops fall into the cold air near the surface, they don't recrystallize into snow, but rather form frozen pellets, or tiny balls, of ice. Sleet accumulates on the ground much in the same way that snow does, but accumulation rates are much lower.

Meteorologists use *liquid equivalent precipitation* in order to explain this phenomenon. When a core of snow or other frozen precipitation is measured and allowed to melt into liquid form, we can measure how much liquid content is in that snowfall. A general rule of thumb is the 10-to-1 ratio, meaning that every 10 inches of snow melts down into one inch of liquid-equivalent precipitation. High snow-to-liquid ratios equate to high snowfall totals. Lake-effect snow, for example, can have snow-to-liquid ratios as high as 30-to-1 or 40-to-1. Sleet, on the other hand, has a very low snow-to-liquid ratio, as low as 3-to-1. The bane of every forecaster who is trying to forecast snowfall amounts is when snowfall mixes with sleet or changes over entirely. This can result in a bust of a snowfall forecast and disappointed schoolchildren all across the land.

Freezing rain, or glaze, occurs in a similar vertical temperature profile to sleet. A warm layer under the cloud allows for partial or total melting of precipitation. The difference between freezing rain and sleet is that the cold air is a very shallow or thin layer right at the ground. Falling precipitation does not have time to completely refreeze into sleet, but rather remains in liquid form. These liquid drops come into contact with below-freezing objects on the ground—sidewalks, trees, and power lines—and freeze on contact. Freezing rain can be a very high-impact hazard, and an ice storm can result in downed power lines and lengthy power outages. Freezing rain can be measured radially, by its accumulation across tree branches or power lines, or as "flat ice," on a flat surface. Power outages can occur with as little as 0.25 inches of flat ice. The National Weather Service will issue a Freezing Rain Advisory or an Ice Storm Warning, depending on how much ice accumulation is expected.

Hail is noteworthy for being the only type of frozen precipitation that falls out of thunderstorms, and thus can occur in any season. Hail forms in the updrafts of energetic thunderstorms. As a hailstone is lofted upward into a storm on strong updrafts, supercooled water (liquid water that is below the freezing point) accretes onto the stone. The hailstone can repeatedly rise upward and fall downward

Photo 28: Three-inch hailstones. Image courtesy: W. Reeves/NOAA Photo Library.

in a storm cloud, leading to the appearance of concentric rings when it is viewed in a cross section. As hailstones rise and fall in a cloud, they can grow extremely large; the largest hailstone on record in the United States fell in Vivian, South Dakota in 2010 (Photo 28). It measured an impressive eight inches in diameter and weighed nearly two pounds! Even small hail of a half inch diameter can do damage to outdoor structures, cars, and more.

Rime doesn't come to mind first when thinking about precipitation types, but it can be breathtakingly beautiful and is worth a mention. When clouds or fog are present and the tiny cloud droplets are supercooled, they collide with surfaces and freeze on contact. As the tiny cloud drops accrete on surfaces, they create delicate, feathery ice protrusions that point in the upwind direction, where the wind is coming from. Rime ice can occur frequently at mountain summits, where supercooled cloud drops are often present. This type of precipitation is generally light in nature, but heavy riming can occur with the right conditions, as in Photo 29, from the Mount Washington Observatory.

Photo 29: Heavy rime ice covering surfaces at the Mount Washington Observatory, on the summit of Mount Washington, NH. Image courtesy: Mount Washington Observatory.

Riming not only occurs on objects that are fixed to the ground, but can also occur as ice crystals fall through a cloud layer comprised of supercooled droplets. As riming occurs on the tiny ice crystals, they lose their crystalline shape and take on the appearance of tiny, round pellets that resemble extremely tiny hailstones or sleet pellets. Known as graupel, these rimed pellets can be very difficult to distinguish from small hail, which can occur in similar conditions.

Autumn Topic #3: Midlatitude Cyclones, Fronts, and Forecasts

Air Masses and Fronts

The ultimate source of energy that drives all of the circulations in Earth's atmosphere is the sun, which heats the earth unequally from equator to poles. The atmosphere is constantly attempting to equalize this heating imbalance by moving cold air to where it is warm, and warm air to where it is cold. When it sits in one place for some time, air tends to take on the characteristics of the type of surface it sits over. *Air masses* are simply large bodies of air that have similar temperature and humidity characteristics throughout. Large northern land masses (such as Northern Canada) tend to generate cold, dry air masses, while northern oceans tend to generate cool, humid air masses. Conversely, warm oceans and land masses tend to generate warm/humid and warm/dry air masses, respectively.

Air masses, once formed, can move from the regions where they are generated. For example, when a cold polar or Arctic air mass moves south from Canada into the United States, the location becomes extremely cold. While *cold* can cover a wide range of temperatures from, say, Houston to Minneapolis, an Arctic air mass can affect both cities with much colder than normal air.

The boundary, or transition zone, between two different air masses is known as a *front*. These boundaries are not smoothly changing temperatures, but rather sharp changes in temperature over short distances. The Norwegian cyclone model, which describes how surface weather systems evolve, was developed by scientists during World War I who used the term 'front' as soldiers were being sent to the front lines of battle, or the dividing line between the two sides. The difference between a battle front and a weather front is that a battle front is defined only right at the surface where the soldiers are, whereas weather fronts actually have three-dimensional characteristics that extend well above the surface, because masses of air have depth and are not flat at ground level.

Types of Fronts

Most weather textbooks describe four basic types of fronts: stationary, warm, cold, and occluded (Figure 27 shows warm, cold, and occluded fronts in a low-pressure system). Cold fronts and warm fronts are defined as the leading edge of the cold or warm air mass, respectively. In other words, behind a cold front, cold air is advancing and the temperature drops after the cold front passes. Conversely, warm fronts, usher in warmer air masses, and the temperature rises after their passage. Stationary fronts are characterized by the presence of a temperature boundary but very little movement of air masses. Occluded fronts form when a cold front overtakes a warm front near the end of the life cycle of a cyclone; more on this in a bit.

The important thing to remember about fronts and air masses is that different air masses have different temperature and density properties. Cold air tends to be denser than warm air, so

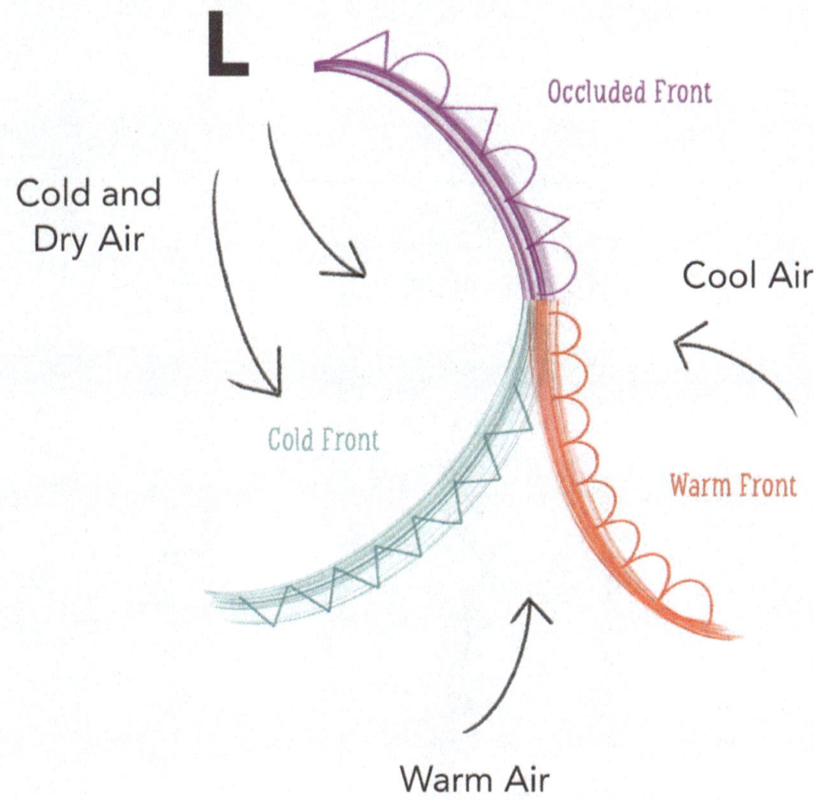

Figure 27

when cold air is replacing warm air, the less-dense warm air is forced upward by the denser cold air. Whenever air is being forced to rise, clouds and precipitation result. Thus, fronts tend to be "weather makers," bringing with them inclement and sometimes high-impact weather. Each of the four types of fronts are typically found in cyclones as they progress through their life cycle.

Life Cycle of a Cyclone

Weather systems (just like everything else in nature) have a life cycle: they are born, evolve into a mature phase, and eventually weaken and die out (Figure 28). Any storm or cyclone requires energy to grow or strengthen. Midlatitude cyclones, such as what we experience here in the United States, derive their energy from temperature contrasts in the atmosphere. Although it may not seem intuitive, fronts in the atmosphere represent sources of potential energy, much like a loaded spring. Just like a loaded spring can be released to convert the pent-up potential energy into kinetic energy, or energy of motion, potential energy at a front can be converted into kinetic energy (wind) given the right ingredients.

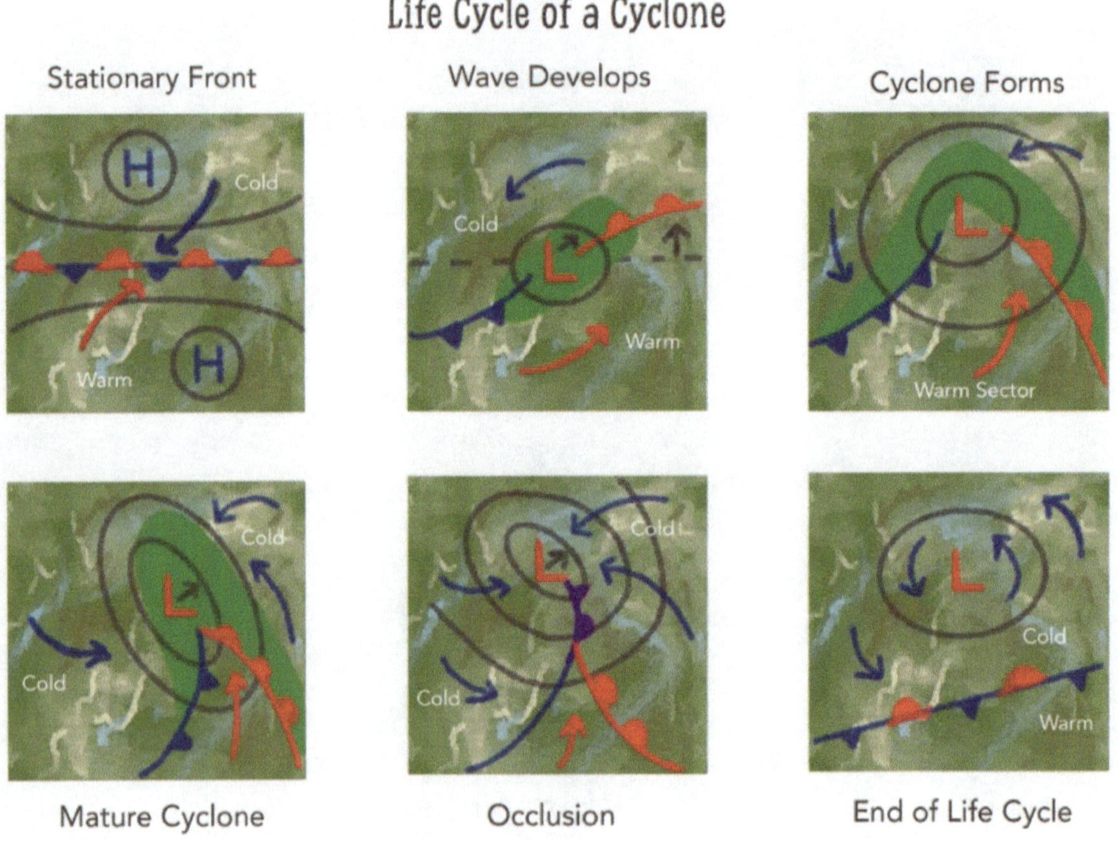

Figure 28

The first stage of the life cycle of any midlatitude cyclone is the presence of a stationary front. Generally speaking, the stronger the front, the more available energy there is. Waves in the jet stream are constantly changing and moving, far above the surface.

In Chapter 3, we talked about how these waves can create areas of upper-level divergence, or spreading out of air. When a wave moves over a front at the surface, that "vacuum" effect causes inflow and counterclockwise rotation at the surface—a low-pressure system is born! As the counterclockwise circulation develops, the previously stationary front begins to advance northward on the east side of the low pressure, while it begins to advance southward on the west side, becoming the warm and cold fronts of the system. Warm air to the south of the system begins to move northward and up over the top of the cold air ahead of the warm front. Similarly, cold, dense air behind the cold front undercuts warm air as it moves southward. Remember that the warmer, less dense air will always be forced up and over the colder, denser air. Once the low pressure has a well-developed warm front and cold front, it has entered the mature phase of its life cycle.

Now let's take a closer look at warm fronts and cold fronts, and the type of weather you might experience with each. Imagine standing at the surface with a warm front approaching you. There are two types of motion occurring: warm air is flooding up and over the top of the colder air where you are standing at the surface, much as if it were on an escalator, while at the same time the front itself is also moving toward you. The first indicator you will see with an approaching warm front is very high, thin cirrus clouds. As the front approaches, clouds will gradually thicken and lower, changing from cirrus to altostratus to low stratus clouds. Eventually, rain or snow may begin falling. Precipitation ahead of a warm front tends to be light or moderate and occur over a fairly wide area. Once the warm front passes by, temperatures increase and the sun may even come out.

As a cold front approaches, warm air is still rising at the front, though the motion is more like an elevator than an escalator. In other words, cold air is forcing warm air upward violently, nearly vertically, just ahead of the front, rather than allowing it to glide gently up over a long horizontal distance. If you were standing in the *warm sector* of the cyclone, where the warmest, most humid air is located, there might be some cumulus clouds, or the sky may be completely clear. As the cold front approaches, there is usually a line of precipitation and/or thunderstorms ahead of the front. Rather than light-to-moderate widespread precipitation that occurs ahead of a warm front, the precipitation ahead of a cold front usually arrives suddenly, can be moderate to heavy in intensity, and lasts for a much shorter duration. Once the cold front passes by, there is a drop in temperatures, a wind shift to the north or northwest, and clearing skies. For gardeners, any rainfall can be beneficial, but warm frontal precipitation tends to be the kind that saturates the soil better, whereas cold frontal precipitation can be so heavy that it runs off rather than sinks into the soil.

As a low-pressure system evolves, airflow around the system in three dimensions moves in a counterclockwise direction. As a cyclone approaches the end of its life cycle, the faster moving cold front catches up to the slower warm front from the center outward, sort of like a zipper. When the cold front catches up to the warm front, an occluded front forms. Weather with an occluded front can be dismal; thick clouds, precipitation ranging from light to heavy, and chilly, damp conditions at the surface. Because of their structure, there isn't always a large temperature contrast on either side of an occluded front at the surface. The formation of an occluded front represents the beginning of the end of a cyclone. Once the occlusion process is complete, all of the warm air in the cyclone is above the surface, with the cold air underneath, and the potential energy has been used up. This life cycle has helped the atmosphere to move warm air toward the poles and cold air toward the equator, thus fulfilling its mission of attempting to equalize the ever-present heating imbalance caused by the sun's energy hitting the tropics more directly than the poles.

It is likely no surprise that there is a huge spectrum of cyclone strengths and intensities, and depending on how strong the cyclone is when it impacts you, where it is in its life cycle, and where you are located with reference to the fronts, the weather you may experience can be drastically different. Strong cyclones can bring blizzard conditions and strong winds, while weaker ones or those with less moisture available may pass with just a few clouds. If the system has a strong cold front, you may experience summer-like conditions and fall- or winter-like conditions in the same day! No two weather systems are ever the same.

The Blizzard of 1888

The Blizzard of 1888 was just one of many high-impact late-season snowstorms in the Northeast. It was significant because of its wide-reaching influence and record-setting snowfall totals. Some of the records from 1888 still stand today, over 130 years later.

Precipitation began in New York City on March 12 as rain, which then changed to snow as the temperature fell. In upstate New York, precipitation was all snow, which persisted through the early-morning hours of March 14.

Strong winds and heavy snow created widespread blizzard conditions, and traffic and commerce were ground to a standstill. The storm brought with it an anomalously cold Arctic air mass that caused temperatures to drop into the single digits, even as far south as New York City.

An estimated 400 people, more than 200 of them in New York City, died. Blowing and drifting snow, even after precipitation had ended, exacerbated cleanup efforts in the days following the storm. Central Park reported 21 inches of snowfall; Saratoga Springs, New York reported the highest statewide storm total snowfall at a whopping 58 inches.

Bennington, Vermont, reported 48 inches of snow, and Middleton, Connecticut, reported 50 inches. The storm broke numerous wind, cold temperature, and snowfall records, and stands today as one of the highest-impact snowstorms to affect the Northeast, a benchmark storm against which other significant storms are measured (73).

Making a Weather Forecast

I know, I know: meteorologists are lucky, they have great jobs and they only have to be right half of the time. But if this discussion about cyclones and their evolution has taught us anything, it is that weather is extremely complex. We have previously talked about all of the instruments and parameters that must be measured accurately in order to measure the current conditions of the atmosphere, as well as all of the physical forces that govern where and how fast the wind blows. I say all of this not to make an excuse for the (hopefully occasional) bad forecast you hear, but to simply point out how far the science of weather forecasting has advanced in even just the past hundred years. Prior to the invention of satellites and radar, it wasn't even possible to see a major hurricane until it was already impacting the coast!

The first necessary step in making a weather forecast is understanding the current state of the atmosphere. All of those weather instruments we discussed are absolutely crucial. And even though we have volumes more information than we did just a few decades ago, it is still not a complete picture of the state of the whole atmosphere. Remember the idea that there is structure of motions on all scales, ranging from around the globe to tiny microscale motions? It is all but impossible to capture some of these tiny features even with our high-tech measuring systems, and the tiny features can accumulate and influence larger-scale motions in the atmosphere that become our weather systems.

The Lorenz Effect

What do butterflies have to do with forecasting the weather?

In 1961, Dr. Edward Lorenz, a professor of meteorology at the Massachusetts Institute of Technology, made a serendipitous discovery that led to the coining of the term butterfly effect. Dr. Lorenz was running a computer simulation and found that a simple rounding difference in the thousandths place resulted in an entirely different weather pattern by the end of the two-month simulated forecast period.

The idea behind the butterfly effect is that tiny, imperceptible changes in initial conditions of a simulation can result in different solutions, and that these tiny differences amplify over time. Lorenz surmised that a butterfly flapping its wings might eventually have an upscale effect that results in a tornado somewhere else in the world. His findings suggested that there was a limit to the accuracy of weather forecasts (especially past the 15-day mark), simply based on the tiny errors in observations that occur routinely as a result of sensitivity of equipment, location of sensors, and many other factors.

The butterfly effect is one aspect of the larger chaos theory, which studies unpredictable behavior in systems that are governed by a specific set of laws. Today, advances in modeling techniques, along with higher resolution and more precise observations, have drastically improved the quality of numerical weather forecasts from the early days in the middle of the twentieth century (74).

The advent of powerful supercomputers has allowed the field of numerical weather prediction, or computer weather forecasting, to advance by leaps and bounds. In short, the computer reads all of the weather data from the surface through the upper atmosphere. That data is then interpolated to a uniform grid the computer can use. Once that step is complete, the physics equations that govern the motions of the atmosphere are "stepped forward" in tiny increments of time. Each step forward is used to compute the next forecast.

There are potential errors at every step of the process: each type of weather instrumentation has limitations, and the interpolation of weather data to a grid and the simplification of physics equations that make the data usable by computers can add errors. These multiply over time, which is why there is an inherent limit to how detailed or accurate the forecast can be with increasing time. There is also the limitation of how fast computers need to be in order to churn through complex physics equations and produce usable information in a reasonable amount of time. Early computers were so slow that the physics equations had to be greatly simplified and grid-point spacing had to be very coarse (widely spaced) just so that the computer could, for example, produce a 12-hour forecast in less than a 12-hour time period! However, even these early computers worked much faster than a human doing the same task by hand.

As computers have become increasingly powerful, more and more detail is available in a shorter time frame. Additionally, models can be run multiple times for each forecast period, with small tweaks to the initial input conditions. This technique, called *ensemble forecasting*, allows forecasters to see a wide range of possible solutions, or forecasts, and can be helpful in conveying the inherent uncertainty in any particular forecast (Photo 30). If there is a great deal of spread among ensemble members, this indicates there is great uncertainty with the forecast, and it may be appropriate to communicate a range of possible solutions to the public.

Finally, the newest advances for making weather forecasts involve machine learning. *Analog forecasting* is a technique that has been used by meteorologists for generations. You may hear a seasoned, experienced meteorologist say something like, "This storm could be very similar to the Blizzard of 1888," for example. The forecaster is reviewing in his or her memory all of the storms he or she has experienced or made a forecast for, and determining which, if any, have similarities in structure to the current weather forecast. Today, machine learning can be used to create an analog forecast much faster than any human could. Computers can pore through thousands of data points for past weather conditions, and quickly find the closest analogs to what the current situation is.

Weather forecasting has made dramatic advances even in my career, and it is exciting to see how cutting-edge techniques are being developed to help convey information to the public and decision-makers. In fact, the problem today is that there is often too much information available. Even a trained meteorologist does not have enough time to analyze all available weather data, review every available forecast model and all of its possible solutions, and then synthesize that information into a forecast that is helpful and useful to all possible users. Today's meteorologists must not only be able to analyze all of the incoming data and information, but also must be skilled communicators, helping people and organizations make decisions that can range from small (should I plant my tomatoes this weekend?) to life-saving (should we institute a mandatory evacuation in a major city in advance of an approaching hurricane?).

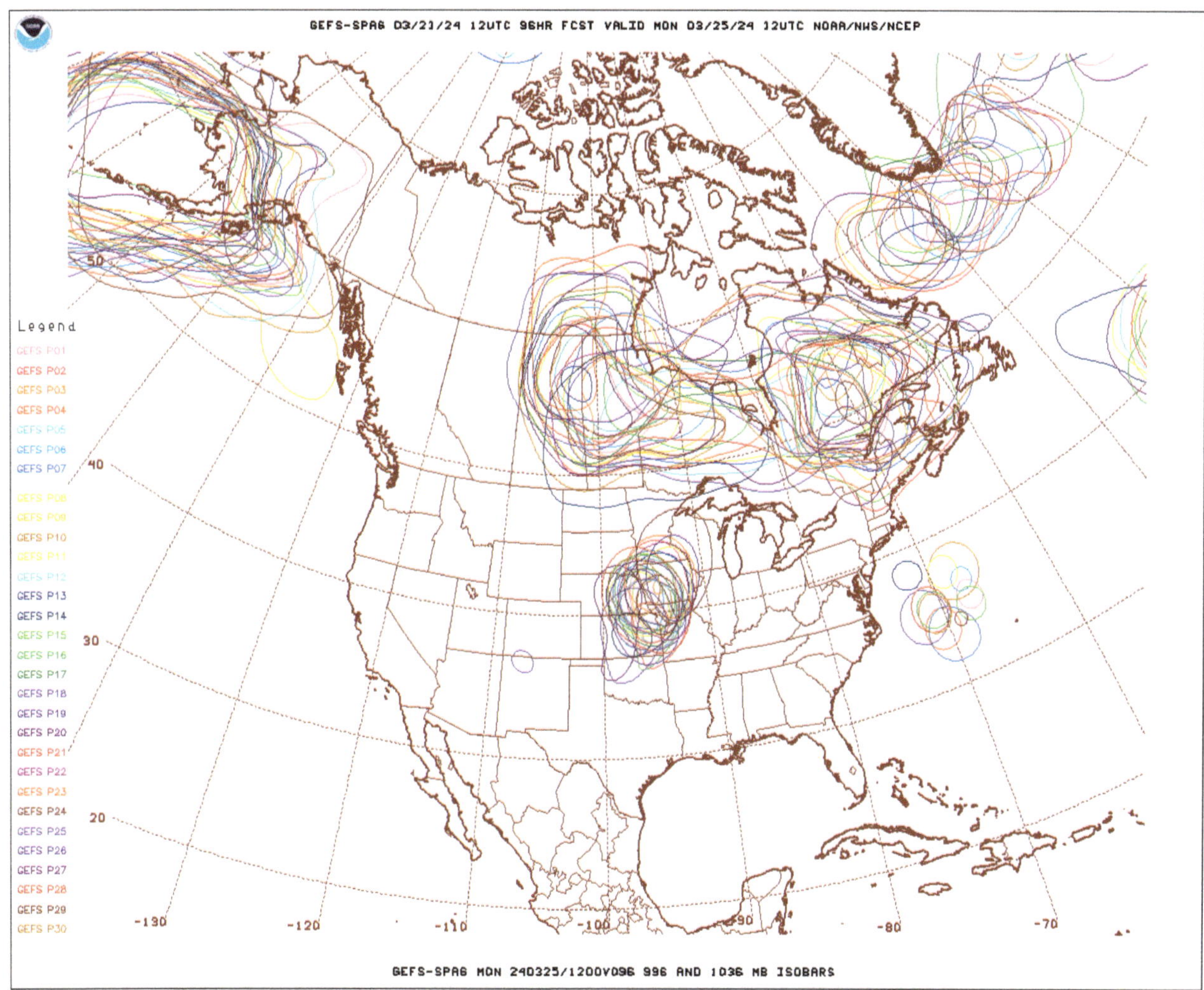

Photo 30: NOAA Global Forecast System (GFS) model ensemble forecast. Colored loops over the Midwest and off the East Coast represent forecast locations of low pressure systems for different ensemble members. The ensemble members are generally in agreement over the Midwest, while there is greater uncertainty off the East Coast.

Autumn Topic #4: Climate and Climate Change

Climate Change: What We Know

While I could write a whole book on climate and climate change, we'll go over the basics of climate, how the Earth's climate changes due to natural phenomena, and human-induced climate change. As we discussed in Chapter 2, *climate* describes the long-term or average conditions that describe a particular location. The standard meteorological climate period is 30 years. To put it very simply, the temperature of the Earth, averaged over the entire year over the whole globe, is governed by a series of inputs, primarily incoming solar radiation, and outputs, such as outgoing Earth radiation.

Think of it this way: Your bank account balance on a particular day represents the cumulative sum of all of the inputs and outputs to the account. If you withdraw more money than you put in, the balance decreases. If you deposit more money than you withdraw, the balance goes up. Just like a bank account, if there is an increase in incoming radiation or a smaller amount of outgoing radiation, the balance, or globally averaged temperature, will go up. The globally averaged temperature would likewise decrease if there was less incoming radiation from the sun, or more outgoing radiation from the Earth.

The WMO defines *climate change* as "a statistically significant deviation in either the mean state of the climate or in its variability, persisting for an extended period, typically decades or longer" (75). These long-term changes can occur for any reason and still be considered climate change. First, we will look at the so-called natural variability, or the many reasons that the Earth's climate can change over time without any human influence.

Any change (increase or decrease) in solar output is going to have an effect on the Earth's climate, because the primary source of incoming energy is from the Sun. Sunspot cycles are one factor that can temporarily change solar output. Sunspots run on an approximately 11-year cycle, and while small, these changes in solar output have been shown to have an effect on the Earth's climate (76). However, as we will see shortly, larger changes have been observed than what can be explained by sunspot activity or solar output alone.

When we discussed the seasons in Chapter 1, we looked at how the Earth revolves around the sun in a nearly circular orbit, and also spins or rotates on its axis. It is a bit more complicated than this. In the early 1900s, Serbian scientist Milutin Milankovitch developed a theory that there are three cyclical variations that change the amount of solar energy reaching the Earth (77). First, the shape of the Earth's orbit does not remain constant but oscillates slightly over time. This would result in small, but detectable, changes in the distance between the Earth and the sun. The second, known as *obliquity*, refers to the change in the tilt of the Earth's axis. In general-education meteorology classes, it is typically taught that this tilt is 23.5 degrees, but in reality the Earth's tilt varies over about a 41,000 year period between 22.1 and 24.5 degrees. The larger the angle of tilt, the more exaggerated the seasons would be and the more of the sun's radiation would be received at the poles. Those changes to the distribution of solar radiation allow for changes of climate at both the equator and the poles. The final cyclical change is *axial precession*, or wobble. The Earth's axis has some natural wobble to it, much like a toy top does as it spins. The cycle length is about 26,000 years, and the net result is that this causes variability in climate between the Northern and Southern hemispheres. Because each Milankovitch cycle operates over a different time period, the way in which all three cycles interact is constantly changing, as is the net effect on the Earth's climate.

Changes in the Earth's albedo can also change the solar input to the Earth's surface. Most notably, large volcanic eruptions can spew tons of ash and dust far into the atmosphere. This dust is then transported around the globe on air currents. One not-too-distant example of this was the eruption of Mt. Pinatubo in the Philippines in 1991. Thanks to satellite and other technology, the changes in concentration of aerosols and debris in the atmosphere was measurable, as was the measurable decrease in the Earth's temperature during the following year (78). I remember seeing some incredible sunsets in the weeks and months after the eruption, and I was surprised to learn that an event on the other side of the world could have such a visible effect where I lived!

Any discussion of climate change would be incomplete without discussing anthropogenic, or human-induced, changes to the Earth's climate. Let's start with what we know based on our understanding of atmospheric processes and what we have observed in the long-term climate record. Only with a solid understanding of the knowns can we then move forward and understand what the climate models are projecting for the future.

Back in Chapter 1, we discussed how the greenhouse effect allows life on earth to exist. Without greenhouse gasses on the planet, temperatures would be too cold to support life. We know based on measurements at many locations on earth that levels of carbon dioxide, a greenhouse gas, have been exponentially increasing in the atmosphere since the industrial revolution (79). Interestingly, the carbon dioxide record also shows an annual pattern of increases and decreases, superimposed on top of the long-term increasing trend. This is because the many trees on earth act as a sink, or absorber, of carbon dioxide during periods when photosynthesis is occurring (warm season months). Simply put, plants "inhale" carbon dioxide through photosynthesis, and "exhale" oxygen into the atmosphere—exactly the opposite of what humans do. When the deciduous trees lose their leaves in the fall and winter, photosynthesis markedly decreases, and there is an uptick in atmospheric carbon dioxide levels.

By congressional mandate, the U.S. Global Change Research Program must deliver a report to Congress and the President to synthesize current research, observations, and findings on both human-induced and natural climate change. The most recent Fifth National Climate Assessment (NCA5) was released in November 2023 (22). Topics covered include agriculture, energy, water, transportation, economics, and more. Findings are broken down by region and cover all of the U.S., and several of the assessment's chapters discuss recommendations on responses to the trends and findings discussed in the report.

The report notes that the impacts of human-induced climate change resulting from exponentially increasing input of carbon dioxide into the atmosphere are already being felt in some areas of the country, but that reducing carbon dioxide emissions or removing carbon dioxide from the atmosphere will reduce risks and impacts in the future. The report notes that there have been measurable changes to the climate in all areas of the country, for example:

- Warming has occurred in every region in the U.S.
- The frequency of overnight minimum temperatures above 70 degrees Fahrenheit is increasing in nearly every region except in Alaska and the Northern Great Plains.
- Heavy precipitation events are increasing everywhere except in Hawaii and the U.S. Caribbean.
- Relative sea levels are increasing in many coastal areas.

There are numerous recommended actions in the report that would help decrease carbon dioxide levels in an effort to work toward reversing the problems and impacts caused by human-induced climate change. Recommendations include expansion of wind and solar energy; use of low-carbon fuels such as hydrogen for transportation; building and designing more energy efficient buildings, appliances, and lighting options; and using urban planning, land management, and building design that reduces demand for energy usage.

As a gardener, you may be asking: "Is there anything I can do to be a good steward of the environment right in my backyard?" The answer is yes! Simple action items include:

- As much as possible, plant native, non-invasive plants in your gardens.
- Use drip irrigation or soaker hoses instead of sprinklers, with a timer and adjustments for natural rainfall, to minimize water evaporation.
- Collect roof runoff water in a rain barrel to use for watering plants.
- Try to minimize the use of gas powered mowers, leaf blowers, and other equipment.
- Pull weeds by hand rather than using chemicals.
- Mulch your lawn clippings rather than collecting; it is good for your lawn!
- Start a compost pile and use it to fertilize your garden.
- Plant trees which will help to shade your home during the summer.

The USDA Plant Hardiness Zone Map

One of the most frequently used maps by home gardeners is the USDA Plant Hardiness Zone Map (PHZM). The hardiness zone map is created based on the lowest daily minimum temperature recorded in any given year at a location to assess 'how cold is the coldest cold that can be expected'? Zones are numbered starting from the north, so the lowest zone numbers represent colder climates. The zones are based on 10-degree Fahrenheit increments, and several sub-zones of five-degree increments allow for finer detail where necessary.

Beginning in 1990, a 30-year time period was considered because that is the standard averaging period for climatological data. Zones are calculated based on the *average* coldest temperature over the 30-year time period. The Hardiness Zone Map was again updated in 2012, and now most recently in 2023, to reflect updated temperature statistics across the country. Temperature records are obtained from many different networks: National Weather Service Cooperative Observer (COOP), USDA Natural Resources Conservation Snow Telemetry (SNOTEL), and the Remote Automated Weather Station network (RAWS, commonly used for fire weather purposes). The 2023 update now includes a high resolution, interactive map viewer on the USDA website. As a meteorologist and a gardener, I find the new PHZM website extremely useful.

As you might expect, since the 'coldest of the cold' temperatures in many areas of the country are not as cold as in decades past, the 2023 PHZM update reflects a change in zones for many regions. According to a Climate Central study of 242 locations across the United States, annual coldest temperatures have increased by an average of seven degrees Fahrenheit since 1970 (42). Near where I live in Albany, New York, the coldest temperature of the year has increased nearly 13 degrees Fahrenheit since 1970. Although it might be logical to conclude that, since I am in a warmer zone, I can grow plants that are less cold-tolerant now, that isn't actually the case.

Recent winters here in upstate New York have been problematic for growers. In both 2023 and 2024, snowfall was below normal until late-season winter storms brought snow, cold, and other impacts during March. Further back in time, March 2018 was plagued by repeated bouts of Arctic cold and three storms which brought accumulating snow to much of the Northeast. The point here is that, even if the coldest-cold temperatures are not as cold, *weather* events can and do occur in any year and can wreak havoc on sensitive plants. Perhaps even more so in a warmer climate, gardens with less-tolerant plants can be more susceptible to late-season frosts and freezes. Snow, sleet, and freezing rain can occur even when the temperature is near or just below freezing, so it does not have to be what we could call 'extreme cold' that creates problems. In my lifetime, Albany has seen measurable snow as late as May 18, and below-freezing temperatures as late as May 20 (both occurred in 2002).

As with many subjects, a little knowledge and information can be very helpful in setting us up for success. Armed with the knowledge that I am now in Zone 6a instead of 5b, I will be doing many of the following things on this list below. While all may not be relevant in your specific zone, there are many ideas here that anyone can apply:

- Try planting new plants...with caution. Although I may be tempted to install more plants that I previously could not, I will proceed slowly and see how these new plants withstand the inevitable variations in weather conditions that occur where I live.
- Do not change the planting schedule very much. While it may seem logical to take advantage of early-season warmth to get a head start on gardening, I will not be making any major adjustments to when I start my seedlings inside or when I transplant them outside.
- Stay tuned to the weather forecast, especially early and late in the growing season. Foreknowledge that cold nights or a winter storm will be coming will allow time to prepare and protect sensitive plants with coverings.

In short; while learning how your garden zone may have changed with the 2023 update to the PHZM may lead you to try new varieties of plants in your garden, it is important to proceed slowly, watch closely, and pay close attention to the weather conditions!

Wrap-up: Autumn

I always feel a sense of closure and completeness when I "wrap up" my garden for the winter, and I feel the same about wrapping up the final section of this book. We have covered some very important and relevant weather topics, and you now have a better appreciation for all the details that go into making a weather forecast, especially when mixed precipitation types are involved, and an understanding about how changes in atmospheric greenhouse gasses are impacting our planet.

Gardener Goals

- The next time you see a rainbow in the sky, take note of where the sun is and where the clouds are. If the rainbow is very bright, try to find a secondary rainbow just outside the primary one and look for the inverted colors.
- If you live in a region which experiences winter precipitation, try to determine which precipitation type is occurring during a winter storm if it is not entirely snow.
- If you are part of a gardening club or other local group, reach out to your favorite local broadcast meteorologist and invite them to come and speak. Broadcast meteorologists are trained to be excellent communicators, and the ones who have lived in your area for a long time will be very familiar with local terrain and weather patterns. Alternatively, if you know a private sector meteorologist in your area, reach out to them as well! Many of us offer seminars for community groups for free or at a nominal cost and love being out in the community to answer weather questions!
- Look up your gardening zone on the USDA website and see if it has changed since the 2023 update was completed.

Reflecting on Seasons Passed

Lessons from Nature

In each season, or chapter, of this book, we have examined weather topics of interest to those of us who enjoy the outdoors in our gardens. Although this is not an exhaustive survey of meteorology, we have covered many of the popular or relevant topics which I am asked about during my seminars at gardening groups. No matter what type or level of gardener you consider yourself to be, there is always something to learn by paying close attention to the weather, and long-term changes in weather conditions, at your location.

One way to learn about your local conditions and changes over seasons and time is to take weather observations on your property. I have included an appendix that goes into detail about how to take weather observations. The process can be as simple or complex as you would like, starting from a pencil and paper and going all the way up to an automated backyard weather station. The appendix gives you both basic information for getting started, and some resources to help you determine which level of complexity is right for you.

As we come to a close, I hope that you have learned some interesting facts about how the atmosphere works, gleaned some useful and practical tips to apply in your own garden, and find yourself invigorated to become a more conscious observer of nature in your own backyard. It has been a challenge and a joy for me to connect my love of gardening and my passion for making science applicable and understandable together in this book.

Appendix 1

Backyard Weather Observations

Taking Weather Observations in Your Backyard

If you are interested in taking weather observations where you live, but are not ready to dive into being an official observer in CoCoRaHS or other networks, we will cover some tips to help you get started.

Basic Tools for Weather Observing

You can add complexity as time goes on, but you'll need a few basic items to get started:

- A notebook. Anything will do: a $0.99 composition book from the back-to-school aisle, a pretty journal, or even a legal pad. I recommend something with horizontal lines; you can use a ruler to add vertical lines for various columns as needed. It is also helpful to have a spiral-bound or other type notebook that allows you to open it wide and lays flat, to flip back and forth between pages easily.
- A pen or pencil. What kind is a matter of preference, but choose an ink that will not bleed when wet. I cannot tell you how many times I have written notes after being outside in the garden, and my wet hands have smeared my writing—a particular problem for lefties like me!

Once you get in the habit of taking daily observations, you can periodically enter your data into a spreadsheet or a note on your phone, but I find it easiest to start with the old-fashioned paper and pencil!

If you are starting with a blank notebook and not the template supplied in this book, create a few columns in your notebook: date, time of observation, a column for each parameter you plan to record, and a Notes column where you can write down interesting weather, notes on the timing of precipitation, visual appearance of clouds, and other non-weather observations, including timing of phenology markers such as leaf-out, leaf drop, buds and blooms. Make sure that the Notes column is the widest one, to allow plenty of room for jotting down observations.

Taking your First Weather Observations

While backyard weather observing can become much more complex, it's easiest to start by observing nature. Set aside a time once daily, as close to the same time each day as possible, to make notes about what you see going on around you. Some people like to do this in the morning as they are enjoying the first cup of coffee; for others, it is helpful to reflect on the day's weather after dinner or toward the end of the day. If you are just beginning and have not yet invested in any special equipment, try recording the following information:

- **Date**
- **Time of observation** (don't forget a.m./p.m.)
- **Cloud cover at the time of observation:** Use the following simple categories: overcast, mostly cloudy, partly cloudy, mostly clear, clear. There are specific ways that trained weather observers use these terms, but you don't need to worry about the exact definitions.
- **Temperature:** With no weather equipment to start with, you may simply record "cold," "chilly," "pleasant," "warm," or "hot" (based on your own experience living at your location).
- **Precipitation:** Again, if you are starting with no equipment, simply note the type, intensity, and approximate duration (e.g., "heavy rainfall in the morning," "light snow all day," "flurries but no accumulation").
- **Snowfall:** If there has been accumulating snowfall, you can use a ruler to measure how much, but you will want to familiarize yourself with the guidelines for how to take accurate snowfall measurements (80).
- **Snow depth:** This one is very easy to do if you have a ruler or yardstick, but again be sure to review some basic guidelines about how to do this accurately (81). Hint: record an average over many spots!
- **Sunrise/sunset:** Although you can look up the official sunrise/sunset times, it is always interesting to study how the sun moves in the sky at your location over the course of the year. If you happen to take your daily observations near sunrise or sunset, note markers to remind yourself exactly where the sun is hitting the horizon. Or if you take observations around local noon, try to notice how high up in the sky the sun is and make a note of that. You will notice small changes over the course of the year that relate directly to the Earth's position around the sun and the changing seasons (82).
- **Notes:** In this column, note any other information you may find relevant. Was there a thunderstorm? Wind damage or hail? A rainbow at sunset? An overnight freeze that

glazed up your driveway unexpectedly? Did the leaves on your maple tree start to turn colors? All of these may be helpful as you look back on your record over time, first, to understand your local microclimate, and second, to look for long-term changes over time.

Weather Observing Equipment for the Home Observer

It really IS as simple as getting started with a paper and pen! However, maybe you have been taking observations for some time, and now you are ready to invest in some equipment. Here are a few ideas.

Rain Gauge

The simplest and most economical piece of equipment I would recommend is a rain gauge. While it may be tempting to pick up something at your local nursery or big box store, I suggest investing in an official CoCoRaHS rain gauge even if you don't plan to become part of that volunteer observer network (83). It costs a bit more than a garden-store rain gauge, but will allow you to take accurate measurements, and become a CoCoRaHS observer down the road, if you desire. CoCoRaHS has some excellent guidelines for mounting your rain gauge so you can make sure it isn't blocked by trees and buildings, as well as information about how to read the gauge (84).

Start by taking precipitation measurements once a day at the same time (or as close as possible) each day. If you do decide to become an official observer, you'll want to make your observations in the morning, around approximately 7:00 a.m. local time.

Max/Min Thermometer

If you would like to start taking temperature measurements but are not ready to invest in a full backyard weather station, you can purchase an affordable indoor/outdoor max/min thermometer. While they aren't the most accurate units available, if you carefully set the outdoor component in a shaded, ventilated spot, you can begin to track daily high and low temperatures.

I recommend comparing your observations to a nearby observing location from your local National Weather Service to better understand any biases in your unit. I have one of these simple units at my house, and it generally runs a little bit higher than the official high/low temperatures at the Albany Airport, particularly in the spring, when at certain times of day, it is nearly impossible to prevent the unit from being influenced by direct sun on sunny days.

You can record the daily high and low temperature for each calendar day in your notebook. For example, H58/L42 would indicate a high temperature and low temperature of 58 and 42 degrees. Be sure to read the unit specifications carefully; most units reset at local midnight and start tracking a new max/min after that time.

Backyard Weather Stations

If you are interested in measuring temperature, winds, and other parameters, it is time to invest in a backyard weather station. These can run up to several hundred dollars and beyond, depending on what type you choose, and are a significant step up in cost from the simple items I have listed above. Weather Underground has a helpful guide to purchasing a weather station, with an overview of some of the specifications you may want to look for (85). They also compare and contrast many options on the market. At the time of this publication, LaCrosse, Davis, and Ambient Weather are all good brands to begin your research.

Consider factors such as connectivity, whether you will need a signal booster or repeater to receive information if the unit is wireless, power and mounting equipment, and of course the various types of weather instrumentation that are available. Some brands have software that allows you to keep digital records and more.

Where to Mount Your Backyard Weather Station

Carefully consider the best place to put your weather station to get the most accurate measurements. The National Weather Service has some excellent tips to help you avoid common issues (86). Ideally, you want the station to be mounted in an open area that is free from interference by trees, buildings, and other obstructions (all of which can affect temperature, rainfall, and wind readings). This may involve installing a post in an open area of your property or mounting the unit on a rooftop.

Considerations are different for each weather parameter. For example, temperature measurements should be taken out of direct sunlight, in a ventilated area, and as close to six feet above ground level as possible but not on a blacktop surface. Winds are taken at a standard height of 10 meters (33 feet) above the surface. Even if you mount your sensor on top of your roof, you likely will not be able to reach this height, and thus any wind sensor in a home unit will be susceptible to interference from trees and buildings.

Often, the entire weather station comes as a single unit, and thus sacrifices will have to be made in one type of measurement or another. If you mount your unit on a rooftop, the temperatures will be taken at a much higher elevation than six feet above the ground. But if you mount the unit on a six-foot-high post on the ground, you may sacrifice some quality in the wind measurements. Another consideration is routine maintenance: if ice accretes on your instruments, will you want to climb up on the roof to dislodge it?

Although there is a significant upfront investment and a great deal of research and thought involved when purchasing a home weather station, you will find that you can learn a lot about your local weather simply by studying the output over time. Specifically, you may get hourly or even more frequent weather observations, which will allow you to make notes about features such as timing of sudden temperature shifts (fronts), specific periods of heavy downpours, and thunderstorm wind gusts, which you would not be able to measure directly by simply taking once-daily weather observations.

What to Do with the Information

Once you start taking weather observations, try not to get overwhelmed by the amount of data you have, and remember why you started to begin with: to gain a better understanding of the weather conditions so that you can use the information to make informed decisions about your garden.

Once you've recorded at least a year's worth of data, try taking a look back through the seasons to reflect on what you observed. For me, this happens in the spring, late summer, and late fall. Comparing notes from one season to another, and one year to another, is always informative.

Taking weather observations doesn't have to be complicated, and you will find that the practice encourages you to take time to notice the world around you on a regular basis. You might even decide to become a volunteer weather observer for CoCoRaHS or another network. Meteorologists like me cannot do our jobs without the help of volunteers all over the country who submit temperature, precipitation, and snowfall/snow depth measurements, as well as comments and observations with their reports. I have included a basic weather observation chart on the following pages which you can use to get started.

Weather

Date	Time	Sunrise/ Sunset	Cloud Cover	Precipitation

Notes

Snowfall	Snow Depth	Notes

Appendix 2

Damage Scales

Enhanced Fujita Scale for Tornadoes	
EF Number	Three-Second Gust (miles per hour)
0	65-85
1	86-110
2	111-135
3	136-165
4	166-200
5	Over 200

Saffir-Simpson Scale for Hurricanes		
Category	*Sustained Winds (miles per hour)*	*Types of Damage Due to Hurricane Winds*
1	74-95	**Very dangerous winds will produce some damage:** Well-constructed frame homes could have damage to roof, shingles, vinyl siding, and gutters. Large branches of trees will snap and shallow-rooted trees may be toppled. Extensive damage to power lines and poles likely will result in power outages that could last a few to several days.
2	96-110	**Extremely dangerous winds will cause extensive damage:** Well-constructed frame homes could sustain major roof and siding damage. Many shallowly rooted trees will be snapped or uprooted and block numerous roads. Near-total power loss is expected with outages that could last from several days to weeks.
3	111-129	**Devastating damage will occur:** Well-built frame homes may incur major damage or removal of roof decking and gable ends. Many trees will be snapped or uprooted, blocking roads. Electricity and water will be unavailable for several days to weeks after the storm passes.
4	130-156	**Catastrophic damage will occur:** Well-built frame homes can sustain severe damage with loss of most of the roof structure and/or some exterior walls. Trees will be snapped or uprooted and power poles downed. Fallen trees and power poles will isolate residential areas. Power outages will last weeks to possibly months. Most of the area will be uninhabitable for weeks or months.
5	157 mph or higher	**Catastrophic damage will occur:** A high percentage of frame homes will be destroyed, with total roof failure and wall collapse. Fallen trees and power poles will isolate residential areas. Power outages will last for weeks to possibly months. Most of the area will be uninhabitable for weeks or months.

Acknowledgments

When I started writing this book, I was utterly overwhelmed by the blankness of the page. However, as I started to put thoughts to paper, I was able to visualize what the final manuscript would look like. The journey through writing has, in some ways, been a bit like a journey through a year in my garden. Some parts came easily; other parts required intense thought, research, and rewriting. Other portions were tossed entirely, much like plants that just didn't work out! I have so many people to thank for helping me bring this manuscript to life.

To my editor, Robin Catalano: Thank you so much for encouragement and helpful feedback! Your suggestions and input really helped me to focus my ideas, see where my personal writing style turned into what most would consider 'rambling', and reminded me that good grammar is so important! Your encouraging comments peppered throughout meant so much, and gave me hope that others might find the book engaging as well!

To Stacey Leonard: I am so grateful that you were able to bring my illustration ideas to life! Thank you for the time and personal attention you gave to this project; your illustrations add so much dimension to this book.

To Jan Null and Lourdes Avilés: Thank you so much for being willing to share your incredible photographs with me for use in this book. The skill with which you both capture interesting sky phenomena is second to none!

To Jessika Hazelton and the staff at Troy Book Makers: Thank you for making the whole process of publishing my first book simple and painless! I am so thrilled to have found you right in my backyard- you helped turn this dream into a reality.

To Lyndsay, for reviewing this manuscript: It's been a pleasure to work with you, and I can't thank you enough for being willing to take on this project in your first few months at STM Weather! I look forward to working with you on many more fun projects in the future.

To my very first coworker, Kelly: It is because of you that this idea even became a reality. Thank you for encouraging me to begin, and giving me honest feedback every step along the way. You have been a joy to work with over the past six and a half years. I am grateful to know you.

To my parents: Thank you so much for telling me I could do anything I set my mind to. You always encouraged me to read, work hard, and recognize that it is truly a fortunate person who gets to make a living doing something they love.

To Catherine and John: You guys are the best kids. Thanks for being supportive of Mom trying her best to balance work life and family life. Although work/life balance is always a juggling act, I really feel as though I have it all. I hope seeing me go through this long process of working on this book reminds you both that if you can dream it…you can do it! I love you guys!

To Tom: Thank you for always supporting me and encouraging me on this journey, from owning and growing a small business, all the way to writing this book. While I always wanted to do something crazy like this, I don't think I ever saw myself as an author until I told you about my idea and you said, "That's great!" Your support over the years as I have followed this very nontraditional career path in meteorology has been such a blessing to me. I thank you and love you so much!

List of Figures

List of Tables

List of Photos

References

1. **Gattuso, Reina.** The Italian Immigrants Who Grew Fig Trees in Unlikely Places. *Atlas Obscura.* [Online] 16 Dec 2020. [Cited: 31 Mar 2023.]

2. **Hallac, Carole.** Preserving the Italian Vegetable Garden in America. *La Cucina Italiana.* [Online] 30 Oct 2020. https://www.lacucinaitaliana.com/trends/news/preserving-the-italian-vegetable-garden-in-america?refresh_ce=.

3. **Menniti, Mary.** The Italian Garden Project. [Online] 2020. [Cited: 31 Mar 2023.] https://www.theitaliangarden-project.com/.

4. **Silvestri, Pamela.** Gagootz: What it is and how Staten Island says it. *SILive.com.* [Online] 11 Aug 2015. [Cited: 31 Mar 2023.] https://www.silive.com/cooking/2015/08/gagootz_its_that_time_of_the_y.html.

5. **Britannica.** Fig. *Britannica.* [Online] 2 May 2024. https://www.britannica.com/plant/fig.

6. **Korner, Christian , Mohl, Patrick and Hiltbrunner, Erika.** *Four Ways to Define the Growing Season.* [ed.] Johannes Knops. 8, s.l. : John Wiley and Sons Ltd., Aug 2023, Ecology Letters, Vol. 26, pp. 1277-1292.

7. **Spengler, Teo.** Gardening in the Arctic: Growing Arctic Circle Plants. *Gardening Know How.* [Online] 4 Apr 2021. [Cited: 16 Feb 2024.] https://www.gardeningknowhow.com/special/spaces/arctic-gardening.htm.

8. **Alaska Master Gardeners Anchorage.** Alaska Master Gardeners Anchorage: Welcome to AMGA. [Online] https://www.alaskamastergardeners.org.

9. **University of Alaska Fairbanks.** UAF Cooperative Extension Service. [Online] https://www.uaf.edu/ces/.

10. **Houze, Robert A. and Houze, Rebecca.** Cloud and Weather Symbols in the HIstoric Language of Weather Map Plotters. *Bulletin of the American Meteorological Society.* 2019, Vol. 100, 12, pp. 423-443.

11. **Green Mountain Club.** Mud Season and Hiking in Vermont. [Online] [Cited: 31 Mar 2023.] https://www.greenmountainclub.org/hiking/mud-season/.

12. **National Center for Environmental Information.** March 2018 National Climate Report. [Online] Apr 2018. [Cited: 16 Feb 2024.] https://www.ncei.noaa.gov/access/monitoring/monthly-report/national/201803.

13. **Davitt, John.** NY1.com. [Online] 20 Jun 2021. [Cited: 16 Feb 2024.] https://ny1.com/nyc/all-boroughs/weather/2021/06/16/spring-stats-show-that-nyc-had-a-hot-and-dry-spring.

14. **USA National Phenology Network.** USA-NPN Reports. *USA National Phenology Network.* [Online] https://www.usanpn.org/about/reports.

15. **Wessels Living History Farm.** Crop Rotation. *Wessels Living History Farm.* [Online] 23 Sep 2022. https://livinghistoryfarm.org/farminginthe30s/crops_10.html.

16. **National Oceanic and Atmospheric Administration.** The Black Sunday Dust Storm of April 14, 1935. *NOAA/National Weather Service.* [Online] https://www.weather.gov/oun/events-19350414.

17. **State Historical Society of Iowa.** Dust Bowl. *State Historical Society of Iowa.* [Online] https://history.iowa.gov/history/education/educator-resources/primary-source-sets/dust-bowl.

18. **University of Nebraska/National Drought Mitigation Center.** The Dust Bowl. *University of Nebraska/National Drought Mitigation Center.* [Online] https://drought.unl.edu/dustbowl/#:~:text=Although%20it%20technically%20refers%20to,entire%20nation%20during%20the%201930s.

19. **U.S. Drought Monitor.** U.S. Drought Monitor - Current. *U.S. Drought Monitor.* [Online] https://droughtmonitor.unl.edu/CurrentMap.aspx.

20. **Moulton, Madison.** Epic Gardening. [Online] 5 Oct 2023. [Cited: 31 Mar 2023.] https://www.epicgardening.com/rose-of-sharon-vs-hibiscus/.

21. **National Oceanic and Atmospheric Administration.** Climate. *NOAA/National Weather Service.* [Online] https://www.weather.gov/wrh/climate?wfo=bis.

22. **U.S. Global Change Research Program.** *The Fifth National Climate Assessment.* Washington, DC : U.S. Global Change Research Program, 2023. Report.

23. **Pepin, Marie-Helene.** Meteorological observations over the past centuries. *Encyclopedia of the Environment.* [Online] 5 Mar 2019. [Cited: 31 Mar 2023.] https://www.encyclopedie-environnement.org/en/air-en/meteorological-observations-over-past-centuries/.

24. **Moliner, Marianne.** Meteorological observations over the past centuries. *Encyclopedia of the Environment.* [Online] 3 May 2019. [Cited: 31 Mar 2023.] https://www.encyclopedie-environnement.org/en/air-en/meteorological-observations-over-past-centuries/.

25. **National Oceanic and Atmospheric Administration, Department of Defense, Federal Aviation Administration, U.S. Navy.** Automated Surface Observing Systems (ASOS) User Guide. [Online] March 1998. [Cited: 31 Mar 2023.] https://www.weather.gov/media/asos/aum-toc.pdf.

26. **Museo Galileo.** Thermoscope. *Museo Galileo.* [Online] https://catalogue.museogalileo.it/object/Thermoscope.html.

27. **Van Helden, Al.** Santorio Santorio. *The Galileo Project.* [Online] http://galileo.rice.edu/sci/santorio.html.

28. **Princeton University.** Weather Instruments. *The Papers of Thomas Jefferson.* [Online] https://jefferson-weather-records.org/node/40577.

29. **Beauchamp, Zack.** Why Americans still use Fahrenheit long after everyone else switched to Celsius. *Vox.* [Online] 4 Jun 2015. [Cited: 31 Mar 2023.] https://www.vox.com/2015/2/16/8031177/america-fahrenheit.

30. **Meteored.** Leonardo da Vinci: A genius who contributed to meteorology. *Yourweather.co.uk.* [Online] 17 Apr 2021. [Cited: 15 Mar 2024.] https://www.yourweather.co.uk/news/science/leonardo-da-vinci-a-genius-who-contributed-to-meteorology.html.

31. **National Oceanic and Atmospheric Administration.** *National Weather Service Instruction 10-1401.* National Weather Service, National Oceanic and Atmospheric Administration. 2010. p. 208, Manual.

32. —. The National Weather Service at 150: A Brief History. *NOAA/National Weather Service.* [Online] 6 Feb 2020. [Cited: 31 Mar 2023.] https://vlab.noaa.gov/web/nws-heritage/-/the-national-weather-service-at-150-a-brief-history.

33. —. About Our WSR-88D Radar. *NOAA/National Weather Service.* [Online] https://www.weather.gov/iwx/wsr_88d.

34. —. NWS Dual Pol Doppler Radar: Rain vs. Snow. *NOAA/National Weather Service.* [Online] https://www.weather.gov/lmk/nws_radar_dualpol_rainsnow.

35. **EarthNetworks.** Total Lightning Network. *EarthNetworks.* [Online] [Cited: 31 Mar 2023.] https://www.earthnetworks.com/why-us/networks/lightning.

36. **National Oceanic and Atmospheric Administration.** Severe Weather 101 - Lightning. *NOAA/National Severe Storms Laboratory.* [Online] https://www.nssl.noaa.gov/education/svrwx101/lightning/detection.

37. **Vaisala.** National Lightning Detection Network. *Vaisala.* [Online] https://www.vaisala.com/en/products/national-lightning-detection-network-nldn.

38. **National Oceanic and Atmospheric Administration.** NWS Cooperative Observer Program. *NOAA/National Weather Service.* [Online] https://www.weather.gov/coop/overview.

39. **Community Collaborative Rain, Hail and Snow Network.** CoCoRaHS - Community Collaborative Rain, Hail and Snow Network. [Online] [Cited: 31 Mar 2023.] https://www.cocorahs.org/.

40. **World Meteorological Organization.** WMO Guildelines on the Calculation of Climate Normals. *World Meteorological Organization.* [Online] https://library.wmo.int/doc_num.php?explnum_id=4166.

41. **National Centers for Environmental Information.** U.S. Climate Normals. [Online] 2021. [Cited: 31 Mar 2023.] https://www.ncei.noaa.gov/access/us-climate-normals/.

42. **Climate Central.** 2021 Record Rain Days. *Climate Central.* [Online] 10 Nov 2021. [Cited: 31 Mar 2023.] https://www.climatecentral.org/climate-matters/record-rain.

43. —. Warm Summer Nights. *Climate Central.* [Online] 19 Jul 2022. [Cited: 31 Mar 2023.] https://www.climatecentral.org/climate-matters/warm-summer-nights-2022.

44. **Miller, Ronald J.** *State Climate Extremes Memorandum.* Spokane, Washington, NOAA/National Weather Service. 2022. p. 28, Memorandum.

45. **National Oceanic and Atmospheric Administration.** Christmas - Albany, NY (1874-2023). *NOAA/National Weather Service.* [Online] https://www.weather.gov/media/aly/Climate/Christmas_table.pdf.

46. **KATU Staff.** Portland's second longest dry streak comes to an end, five days short of a new record. *KATU.* [Online] 14 Sep 2022. [Cited: 31 Mar 2023.] https://katu.com/news/local/portlands-second-longest-dry-streak-comes-to-an-end-five-days-short-of-new-record-airport-national-weather-service-meteorology.

47. **National Oceanic and Atmospheric Administration.** National Hurricane Center Forecast Verification. *NOAA/National Hurricane Center.* [Online] 7 Jun 2024. https://www.nhc.noaa.gov/verification/.

48. —. NOAA Cloudwise. *NOAA/National Weather Service.* [Online] 19 Aug 2019. [Cited: 15 Mar 2024.] noaa.gov/sites/default/files/2023-03/cloudchart-front.pdf.

49. **Cooperative Institute for Meteorological Satellite Studies.** Low Level Clouds - V. *Satellite Meteorology for Grades 7-12.* [Online] https://cimss.ssec.wisc.edu/satmet/modules/4_clouds/clouds-7.html.

50. **National Oceanic and Atmospheric Administration.** NWS Glossary. *NOAA/National Weather Service.* [Online] 25 Jun 2009. [Cited: 14 Apr 2023.] https://forecast.weather.gov/glossary.php.

51. —. What Are El Nino and La Nina? *NOAA/National Ocean Service.* [Online] 24 Aug 2023. [Cited: 15 Mar 2024.] https://oceanservice.noaa.gov/facts/ninonina.html.

52. **University Center for Atmospheric Research.** Thunderstorms. *UCAR Center for Science Education.* [Online] https://scied.ucar.edu/learning-zone/storms/thunderstorms.

53. **National Oceanic and Atmospheric Administration.** What is a microburst? *NOAA/National Weather Service.* [Online] https://www.weather.gov/bmx/outreach_microbursts.

54. —. Squall Line/Bow Echo/QLCS. *NOAA/National Weather Service.* [Online] https://www.weather.gov/lmk/squallbow.

55. **Corfidi, Stephen F., Evans, Jeffry and Johns, Robbert.** About Derechos. *NOAA - Storm Prediction Center.* [Online] 11 Jan 2022. [Cited: 14 Apr 2023.] https://www.spc.noaa.gov/misc/AbtDerechos/derechofacts.htm.

56. **Ahrens, Donald C. and Henson, Robert.** *Meteorology Today: An Introduction to Weather, Climate, and the Environment.* s.l. : Cengage, 2021.

57. **Larson, Lee W.** The Great USA Flood of 1993. *Northwest River Forecast Center.* [Online] 1996. https://www.nwrfc.noaa.gov/floods/papers/oh_2/great.htm.

58. **National Oceanic and Atmospheric Administration.** Severe Weather 101: Tornado Types. *NOAA/National Severe Storms Laboratory.* [Online] https://www.nssl.noaa.gov/education/svrwx101/tornadoes/types/.

59. **National Weather Service, Goodland, Kansas.** U.S. Lightning Fatalities, 2012-2022. [Online] https://www.weather.gov/images/gld/Lightning/2022/Slide3.JPG.

60. —. Fatal Lightning Incidents by Month. [Online] https://www.weather.gov/images/gld/Lightning/2022/Slide4.JPG.

61. **National Oceanic and Atmospheric Administration.** When a Safe Building or Vehicle is Nearby. *NOAA/National Weather Service.* [Online] https://www.weather.gov/safety/lightning-outdoors.

62. —. Lightning Safety Indoors. *NOAA/National Weather Service.* [Online] https://www.weather.gov/safety/lightning-indoors.

63. —. Major Hurricane Harvey - August 25-29, 2017. *NOAA/National Weather Service.* [Online] 2017. https://www.weather.gov/crp/hurricane_harvey.

64. —. How do hurricanes form? *NOAA/National Ocean Service.* [Online] 20 Jan 2023. [Cited: 14 Apr 2023.] https://oceanservice.noaa.gov/facts/how-hurricanes-form.html.

65. **Emmanuel, Kerry.** Hurricane Potential Intensity Maps. *Kerry Emmanuel.* [Online] 2004. https://emanuel.mit.edu/hurricane-potential-intensity-maps-0.

66. **Kossin, James P.** *Global increase in major tropical cyclone exceedance probability over the past four decades.* 22, Proceedings of the National Academy of Science of the United States of America, Vol. 177, pp. 11975-11980.

67. **National Oceanic and Atmospheric Administration.** NOAA Hurricane Hunters. *NOAA/Office of Marine and Aviation Operations.* [Online] https://www.omao.noaa.gov/aircraft-operations/noaa-hurricane-hunters.

68. **Avila, Lixion A. and Cangialosi, John.** Tropical Cyclone Report Hurricane Irene (AL092011) 21-28 August 2011. *NOAA/National Hurricane Center.* [Online] 2011. https://www.nhc.noaa.gov/data/tcr/AL092011_Irene.pdf.

69. **Coyne, Michael.** *Hurricane Ida Service Assessment.* National Weather Service, National Oceanic and Atmospheric Administration. Silver Spring, MD : s.n., 2023. p. 95.

70. **National Oceanic and Atmospheric Administration.** Winter Weather Topics. *NOAA/National Weather Service.* [Online] https://www.weather.gov/ilx/swop-wintertopics.

71. **Jericho Historical Society.** Snowflake Bentley. [Online] https://snowflakebentley.com.

72. **Libbrecht, Kenneth.** Snow Crystals. *Snowcrystals.com.* [Online] http://snowcrystals.com/.

73. **Burt, Christopher C.** The Blizzard of 1888: America's Greatest Snow Disaster. *Weather Underground.* [Online] 2020. https://www.wunderground.com/cat6/the-blizzard-of-1888-americas-greatest-snow-disaster..

74. **Dizikes, Peter.** When the Butterfly Effect Took Flight. *MIT Technology Review.* 22 Feb 2011.

75. **World Meteorological Organization.** Climate. *World Meteorological Organization.* [Online] [Cited: 16 Feb 2024.] https://wmo.int/topics/climate.

76. **Herring, David.** Couldn't the Sun be the cause of global warming? *Climate.gov.* [Online] 29 Oct 2020. [Cited: 16 Feb 2024.] https://www.climate.gov/news-features/climate-qa/couldnt-sun-be-cause-global-warming.

77. **Graham, Steve and King, Hailey.** Milutin Milankovitch. *NASA Earth Observatory.* [Online] 2000 Mar 24. [Cited: 16 Feb 2024.] https://earthobservatory.nasa.gov/features/Milankovitch.

78. **NASA Earth Observatory.** Global Effects of Mount Pinatubo. *NASA Earth Observatory.* [Online] 14 Jun 2001. [Cited: 16 Feb 2024.] https://earthobservatory.nasa.gov/images/1510/global-effects-of-mount-pinatubo.

79. **National Oceanic and Atmospheric Administration.** Climate Dashboard. *Climate.gov.* [Online] 17 Jun 2022. [Cited: 16 Feb 2024.] https://www.climate.gov/media/14603.

80. **Palecki, Michael.** "In Depth" Snow Measuring. *Community Collaborative Rain, Hail and Snow Network.* [Online] https://media.cocorahs.org/docs/MeasuringSnow2.1.pdf.

81. —. Winter Weather Measurements. *Community Collaborative Rain, Hail and Snow Network.* [Online] 5 Nov 2022. [Cited: 5 May 2023.] https://media.cocorahs.org/docs/WinterPrecipitationMeasurements_V3.0_Nov2022.pdf.

82. **National Oceanic and Atmospheric Administration.** NOAA Solar Calculator. *NOAA Global Monitoring Laboratory/Earth Systems Research Laboratories.* [Online] [Cited: 5 May 2023.] https://gml.noaa.gov/grad/solcalc.

83. **Weather Your Way.** Weather Your Way Gauge Parts. *Weather Your Way: The Official Dealer for CoCoRaHS.* [Online] [Cited: 5 May 2023.] https://weatheryourway.com/collections/cocorahs-gauge-parts.

84. **Community Collaborative Rain, Hail and Snow Network.** Measuring Rain: How to Read Your Rain Gauge. *Community Collaborative Rain, Hail and Snow Network.* [Online] https://www.cocorahs.org/Content.aspx?page=measurerain.

85. **Weather Underground.** Personal Weather Station Buying Guide. *Weather Underground.* [Online] https://www.wunderground.com/pws/buying-guide.

86. **National Oceanic and Atmospheric Administration.** Personal Weather Station - Siting. *NOAA/National Weather Service.* [Online] 13 Aug 2016. [Cited: 5 May 2023.] https://www.weather.gov/media/epz/mesonet/CWOP-Siting.pdf.